MORAL EXPERIMENT IN JACOBEAN DRAMA

MORAL EXPERIMENT IN JACOBEAN DRAMA

T. F. Wharton
Associate Professor of English
Augusta College, Georgia

St. Martin's Press   New York

First published in the United States of America in 1988

Printed in Hong Kong

ISBN 0–312–01331–0

Library of Congress Cataloging-in-Publication Data
Wharton, T.F.
Moral experiment in Jacobean drama / T.F. Wharton
p.   cm.
Bibliography: p.
Includes index.
ISBN 0–312–01331–0 : $30.00 (est.)
1. English drama—17th century—History and criticism.
2. Ethics in literature.
3. Moral conditions in literature.   I. Title.
PR678.E85W48 1988
822'.3'09353—dc 19   87–19689

To My Parents

To My Parents

Contents

Acknowledgements   viii

Introduction   1

1 Chapman   6

2 Disguised Dukes: *The Malcontent*, and *Measure for Measure*   23

3 *The Revenger's Tragedy*   44

4 *The White Devil*   57

5 *The Duchess of Malfi*   74

6 *'Tis Pity She's a Whore*   91

7 Shakespeare   110

Conclusion   133

Notes   137

Index   148

Acknowledgements

Portions of the Introduction have appeared in more extended form in my essay, '"Yet I'll Venture": Moral Experiment in Early Jacobean Drama', *Salzburg Studies in English*, 95 (1980) pp. 3–17. Parts of Chapter 5 have appeared in slightly different form in my essay in the same issue of *Salzburg Studies* (pp. 18–33), '"Fame's Best Friend": Survival in *The Duchess of Malfi*'. Chapter 2 draws heavily on my essay, '*The Malcontent* and 'Dreams, Visions, Fantasies''', *Essays in Criticism*, XXIV (1974) pp. 261–74; and on a second, 'Old Marston or New Marston: the *Antonio* Plays', *Essays in Criticism* XXV (1975) pp.357–69). I gratefully acknowledge the editors' permission to reprint this material.

I acknowledge with thanks the year's study leave granted to me by Glasgow University; and the resources, the congeniality, and the ever-helpful staff of the Folger Shakespeare Library, where I largely spent it.

Finally, to the patience and good judgement of my colleague and dear wife, Rosemary DePaolo, I owe an enormous debt.

T.F.W.

Introduction

When George Whetstone, in 1578, excoriated the modern dramatist, he did so in these terms: 'he first groundes his work on impossibilities; then in three howers ronnes he throwe the worlde, marryes, gets Children, makes Children men, men to conquer Kingdomes, murder Monsters, and bringeth Gods from Heauen, and fetcheth Diuels from Hel'.[1] His criticisms were aimed, in effect, at what we still legitimately think of as one of the key characteristics of the Renaissance mind: the willingness to think in terms of superlative possibilities. Whetstone's modern dramatist sounds rather endearing, in his innocent assumption that so much is possible; that lands are there to be conquered, gods and devils there to be summoned, and the world there to be run through. It is an idea of human drama that reached its peak, in England, in the defeat of an Armada or in *Tamburlaine the Great*. However, even Marlowe's subject matter shrinks down to a pederast weakling King, his beard shaved in puddle-water in a dungeon; and the last years of the century seem altogether to dwindle in spirit to paralysis and introspection, of which *Hamlet* provides the outstanding example.

The key spokesman of this period is Montaigne, whose *Essays* were published in France in the 1580s, and translated into English when England was ready for them (1599–1603). Montaigne was not short of that other recognizable trait of Renaissance man: individualism. Chapter 2 of the third and last book of essays acknowledges that by some standards he may be thought to 'speake too much of [him]self'. His excuse is 'that never man handled subject he understood or knew better than I doe this I have undertaken, being therein the cunningest man alive'.[2] For Montaigne, however, the self is neither assertive nor adventurous. It is simply the only certain knowledge he has. All other knowledge is in doubt: 'If that which the Epicurians affirme be true, that is to say, we have no science if the apparances of the senses be false, and that which the Stoicks say, if it is also true that the senses apparences are so false as they can produce us no science; we will conclude at the charges of these two great Dogmatist Sects, that there is no science'.[3] The essays go on to demonstrate the treachery of the senses, the impossibility of any certain knowledge, and the shallowness of the Renais-

1

sance pride in human possibility. Only the self has any certainty. However, Montaigne also writes of the insecurity of even that self:

> All contrarieties are found in her, according to some turn or removing, and in some fashion or other; shamefast, bashfull, insolent, chaste, luxurious, peevish, pratling, silent, fond, doting, laborious, nice, delicate, ingenious, slow, dull, froward, humorous, debonaire, wise, ignorant, false in words, true-speaking, both liberal, covetous, and prodigall. All these I perceive in some measure or other to bee in mee, according as I stirre or turne my self; And whosever shall heedfully survey and consider himself, shall finde this volubility and discordance to be in himselfe, yea and in his very judgement. I have nothing to say entirely, simply, and with soliditie of myselfe, without confusion, disorder, blending, mingling, and in one word, Distinguo is the most universall part of my logicke.[4]

For Montaigne the answer to such a problematic condition lay in religion. Others shared the problem, but not the solution, and until seventeeth-century science provided another kind of certainty, this seemed to be the condition to which the most thoughtful and contemplative minds seemed temporarily doomed.

Occasionally, however, a new impetus can come, not from philosophy or science, but from art or literature; and occasionally, too, it can come from one specific medium. On this occasion, that medium was drama: not poetry, which, for all the claim of its subsequent title to be 'metaphysical', explores in its far-fetched comparisons only the hallowed and comforting traditional correspondences, perceived as uniting the different parts of the universe. Herbert writes, in *Man*, of these correspondences:

> Man is all symmetrie,
> Full of proportions, one limbe to another,
> And all to all the world besides:
> Each part may call the furthest, brother:
> For head with foot hath private amitie,
> And both with moons and tides.

Donne's famous loving compasses trace and stretch across exactly such parallels between remote parts of nature, the world, and man. He performs superlatively the ultimate exercise of an ancient conviction.

Jacobean drama is far more radical, and can be said alone to contribute ideas to break the impasse: not indeed providing solutions, but suggesting new areas of enquiry for the inquisitive minds who become its central figures. That area of enquiry is moral. These plays' protagonists remain as self-focused as Montaigne, and as sceptical of the mind's own stability. However, they turn these negatives to use, to speculate whether any moral limits really exist. The boldest of these plays make their protagonists ask whether, if there is nothing truly stable about their own identity, that means that they are capable of committing all evil, at will. They ask whether what is called conscience will be a sufficient deterrent to committing such evils. They seek direct experimental proof either way. All these plays ask, how real is the virtue in other people; and, again, experimental proof is directly sought, whether in the form of disguised dukes returning to their kingdoms, of chastity tests, or other forms of temptation or trick. Needless to say, in plays so strongly concerned with unstable identity, disguise and role-playing are endemic.

Interpretations of Jacobean drama as an orthodox 'Quest for Moral Order'[5] therefore leave much to be desired, however well-meaning they might be. On any attentive reading, and especially on any viewing, its tone seems far less solemn than this, and its collective impulse far less constructive. One of its most attractive characteristics is the gleefulness with which it plays its dangerous and subversive games, which set at stake the most sacred human bonds and values. The games are far from sophisticated. On the contrary, they seem almost childlike in their curiosity to 'see how far we can go'. But then, the questions posed by a child's curiosity, being unanswerable, are often the most unsettling of all. They are the questions that the greatest of plays sometimes dare to ask: 'Why should a dog, a horse, a rat, have life,/ And thou no breath at all?'[6] Almost without exception, the best Jacobean plays do conduct a consistent kind of moral enquiry, but if the cumulative effect can be called a 'quest', it must be seen as a quest for moral *dis*order. They seek to prove the human condition to be one of fragmentation, not of bonds; to show how – to use *King Lear* again – 'Love cools, friendship falls off, brothers divide . . . and the bond crack'd 'twixt son and father'. Jacobean drama is an experiment in moral anarchy, and the experiment is located in the closest of family ties. To their horror and their joy, the Jacobean dramatists discover that anything is possible.

This motif of experimentation seems to be almost entirely new. It is hardly found at all in Elizabethan drama. There is of course the apparent exception of Doctor Faustus. Here, surely, there is an enquiring mind, determined to 'try the uttermost magic can perform'. Yet, his is not a moral experiment. He repeatedly requests pure scientific knowledge and eventually attains it:

> Learned Faustus,
> To find the secrets of astronomy,
> Graven in the book of Jove's high firmament,
> Did mount him up to scale Olympus' top . . .[7]

However, as a moral being, Faustus is far less ambitious. Though his powers are potentially immense, he can hardly be said to put them to adventurous use. On the contrary, he manages to shock Mephistophilis by the sheer conventionality of one of his early wishes:

> FAUSTUS But leaving this, let me have a wife, the
> fairest maid in Germany, for I am wanton and
> lascivious, and cannot live without a wife.
> MEPHISTOPHILIS How, a wife? I prithee Faustus,
> talk not of a wife . . .
> Marriage is but a ceremonial toy,
> And if thou lovest me think no more of it.[8]

It is hard to think of another Elizabethan play containing even this degree of experimentation, unless we count *Much Ado About Nothing*, and its recreational project to 'bring Signior Benedick and the Lady Beatrice into a mountain of affection the one with the other'.

However, a poem written within two or three years of that play pointed the direction in which drama was to go. The poem was a seventeen-stanza meditation, by the obscure author Thomas Edwards, on the subject of Ovid's story of Cephalus and Procris (*Metamorphoses*, Book VII). It concerns Cephalus's unreasonable fears for his wife's fidelity during an absence. To test it, he returns in disguise, and persistently propositions her until she succumbs. He then indignantly discloses his own identity. The distinctive feature of the story is that it is a test, a trial, which demonstrates the frailty of even an apparently invincible virtue. The enquirer is always likely to find out the worst in human nature, as here. Only one step now separates this story from the kind of material which so engrosses Jacobean drama: that is, that the Jacobean enquirer tends to expect to find the worst in human nature, his own included, and is exhilarated to be proven right.

That step was taken at the death of Elizabeth and the accession of James I. In fact, with a chronological precision which is close to freakish, as soon as there is Jacobean drama, there is a drama of moral experiment. Before 1604, there is none whatever. The first attempts were inevitably somewhat tentative, but they include some major plays. The best known is undoubtedly Shakespeare's *Measure for Measure*, with its abdicating Duke, and his testing of the 'outward-sainted deputy', Angelo: 'hence shall we see,/ If power change purpose, what our seemers be'.[9] The same year – 1604 – saw another 'disguised duke' tragicomedy, Marston's *Malcontent*; and Chapman's heroic play, *Bussy D'Ambois*, which showed distinct signs of wanting to make its protagonist into an experimenter.[10] In the following year came Chapman's comedy, *The Widow's Tears*, with its deployment of the motif of a chastity test, taken from a Latin source. The year after that produced the first of the great tragedies founded on the idea of moral enquiry, Tourneur's *Revenger's Tragedy*. This is admittedly the densest grouping of such plays that the Jacobean age can offer. The drama of moral experiment, being so radical a departure, never became the dominant form, and there were major authors who virtually eschewed it. These include Shakespeare (despite *Measure for Measure*) and Middleton. However, it can still boast the names of Marston, Chapman, Tourneur, Webster, and – a little after the strictly Jacobean period – Ford; and it can also boast these authors' best work. Whatever the local cause which produced the new form, and so curiously located it to coincide with the first months of a new reign, there can be little doubt that Jacobean drama discovered a major new impulse, and that this new impulse generated some brilliant plays.

1
Chapman

There is an anecdote about Ben Jonson which is fascinating in itself, and which offers some insight into the satiric mentality. The story is in the *Conversations with Drummond*, and concerns a Jonsonian prank: 'He can set Horoscopes, but trusts not jn ym, he with ye consent of a friend Cousened a lady, with whom he had made ane apointment to meet ane old Astrologer jn the suburbs, which she Keeped & it was himself disguysed jn a Longe Gowne & a whyte beard at the light of [a] Dimm burning Candle up jn a litle Cabinet reached unto by a Ledder'.[1] Jonson's joke is very close to the on-stage frauds he creates in his own city comedy. Essentially, the shrewd trickster in some sense exploits one of the legion of fools and dreamers that populate a city. Whether or not he wants to get money by the trick, part of his purpose will always be simply to ridicule; to demonstrate his victims' credulity, and to celebrate his own sharply superior realism. He will never be concerned with the act of enquiry, since his assumptions about human nature are already fixed. Rather, he exploits. This is the difference between drama's tricksters and its experimenters. True, it is *The Revenger's Tragedy*, not *Volpone*, which contains the line, 'The world's divided into knaves and fools'.[2] Nevertheless, the Jacobean plays of moral experiment are more open-ended in their assumptions about human nature. They discover their own definitions during the play.

For instance, it is not city comedy but the drama of moral experiment which is more prepared to concede at least the existence of innocence, as its various Castizas, Marias, Isabellas, and Antonios prove. However, the virtuous now have to exist in changed and far less hospitable conditions than hitherto. The condition of every man and woman is essentially a lonely and isolated one. The idea is given repeated hearing in some of the plays' most memorable lines: 'At myself I will begin and end'; 'To see what solitariness is about dying princes'; 'What make I here? these are all strangers to me'. It is an isolation which makes innocence exceptionally vulnerable, when experiments are played with it. There is suddenly no structure of support for it to invoke. Innocence is still capable of survival, but only by extraordinary strength. Ordinary goodness is liable to rapid contamination by its enemies. One solution is obviously to withdraw from the world, though even this is no guarantee of immunity. Another is for innocence to become combative. Here, though, it may run exactly the same eventual risks of being polluted by what it attacks.

Those comedies and tragedies of Chapman which date from the beginning of the Jacobean period provide the perfect demonstration of the perils of innocence. *The Widow's Tears* is the obvious example, since it contains a full-blown successful moral experiment on the heroine. Even the much less corruptible heroine of *The Gentleman Usher*, though, illustrates the fragility of unfortified innocence, and when, in *Bussy D'Ambois*, integrity abandons its lofty isolation for an equally lofty offensive, the results are at best ambiguous. It is the achievement of Chapman (and perhaps also Marston) to establish that innocence is hardly tenable at all. The one remaining step was to create heroes who actually abandon the possession, the protection, or even the pretence of innocence, and who set out instead more or less actively to prove it a fraud or an illusion.

The Gentleman Usher, usually dated between 1602 and 1604, contains some of 'the highest flights of pure poetry in Chapman's comedies'.[3] It has pure-souled lovers, whose passion transcends tyranny and lust. It has high-minded friendship, Christian piety, and self-sacrifice. At the heart of the play is Margaret, loved virtuously by Vincentio, but courted by his Duke/father, whose hostility to his son extends to an attempt on his life. Good and evil are untroubled by any real complexity in the play, and Margaret's obvious course of action, when it seems that Vincentio is dead, is to mourn and die. Here, however, Chapman begins to complicate his simple tale of virtue resisting vice. For Margaret, none of the available ways of committing suicide seems sufficiently painless. After considering sword, poison, and a leap from a high tower, Margaret confesses her fear and decides to thwart the Duke's lust by instead defacing her beauty with a knife. Once again, however, the thought of pain is too much for her. She is about to resign herself to a far less drastic self-mutilation, ruffling her hair – 'Hence, hapless ornaments that adorn'd this head;/ Disorder ever these enticing curls' (V.iii.45–6) – when her aunt makes a helpful suggestion:

> CORTEZA I have an ointment here which we dames use
> To take off hair when it does grow too low

Upon our foreheads, and that, for a need,
If you should rub it hard upon your face
Would blister it and make it look most vilely

(V.iv.53–7)

Margaret gratefully seizes this idea, and duly performs at court in
the role of Defaced Beauty. The effect of her performance is somewhat lessened when a doctor assures her that, with the help of a
well-known preparation, the blisters will get better in three days.
Now, Margaret is a perfectly good and sincere girl, and Corteza is
a most supportive aunt, regarding defacement with a knife:

CORTEZA   That were a cruel deed. Yet Adelasia,
            In Pettie's *Palace of Petite Pleasure*,
            For all the world, with such a knife as this [*produces a
                                                              knife*]
            Cut off her cheeks and nose, and was commended
            More than all dames that kept their faces whole.

(V.iii.32–6)

However, for Margaret, the heroic sterotypes of an earlier,
Elizabethan fiction are altogether too remote to invite imitation.
She has ideals, but she cannot suffer for them. Living in the kind
of corrupt court more familiar in tragedy than in comedy, she is
culturally isolated from the sustenance the example of Adelasia
might once have provided. Instead, she can preposterously bargain
herself down from suicide to spots.

Her comic failure is the more pronounced, because her story is
actually an inverted version of a tale from another Elizabethan
fiction, Sidney's *Arcadia*. There, Argalus, in love with and loved by
Parthenia, has as rival the wicked Demagorus, who first makes an
attempt on his life, and then, determined that no one else should
have Parthenia, disfigures her beauty with poison. The lovers, however, continue to love each other, even when later separated.
Indeed, in Sidney's version, the lovers are all-powerful. They may
be persecuted, but their love transcends mere circumstance. It is
actually 'proved' by circumstance, since Sidney's story makes love
triumphantly surmount the tests it faces. By switching the disfigurement motif, however, Chapman immediately transforms the
heroine's position into one of weakness, despair and fraud.

Interestingly, Sidney's story includes an actual test by Parthenia of Argalus. During their separation, her face is cured by a doctor. Subsequently, she meets Argalus, pretends to be someone else (who is often mistaken for Parthenia), tells him that Parthenia is dead, and offers her own hand in marriage. Courteously, he declines. His heart belongs to Parthenia for life. She then runs into his arms with the line, 'Why, then, Argalus, take thy Parthenia'.[4] Her test of her lover is perfectly legitimate by the standards of romance; in fact, almost a requirement. Such tests give additional piquancy to narratives which already consist of extreme situations, and they afford love a chance to display its qualities of heroic constancy and generosity. Tests are imposed by one lover on the other in the expectation that they will be passed. When a third party imposes the test, the worst that might happen is that the lover's faith may be temporarily shaken. There is, though, no question of the test being in any sense used by author or tester as an experiment in how easily love may be destroyed. The impetus of the genre is to demonstrate the solidity, not the fragility of love. Even the Protean whims of some of Shakespeare's lovers are something that, after a due period of comic enjoyment, the entire machinery of the plays labour to cure and erase. Yet, in Chapman's last comedy, *The Widow's Tears* (usually dated 1605), exactly such a test becomes for his married and devoted lovers a devastating experiment. It all begins with loss of faith. Once provoked by his brother into a grain of doubt about his wife's fidelity, the husband has to find out the truth. In an earlier play, perhaps, he would have used a romantic test to prove the wife innocent. However, Chapman instead produces all the characteristics of an experiment, including even the appalled fascination of the experimenter with what he is finding.[5]

The plot of *The Widow's Tears* is taken – with one major modification – from Petronius' 'novel', *The Satyricon*; specifically from its story of the widow of Ephesus. Chapman's is its first known dramatization. Interestingly, in its original form, it is not really a chastity test. Simply, a stranger rapidly destroys a widow's chaste dedication to her late husband. Chapman makes it into a chastity test, by in a sense crossing it with Ovid's Cephalus and Procris tale. The graveyard soldier who undermines the widow's fidelity, even in her husband's tomb, is made by Chapman to be the husband himself; who, as in Ovid's story, comes to his widow in disguise and tries to seduce her. By conflating two already powerful plots, Chapman produces something far more extreme than that other best-known chastity test in Western literature, *Don Quixote's* story of The Curious

Impertinent. We have not just a husband testing his wife, nor even a disguised husband trying to seduce his own wife; not only a seduction taking place over the body of the dead husband; but a seduction by the husband of his own widow, over his own dead body.

It is evident that Chapman deliberately sought out the most outrageous situation possible. It has all the more impact since, in the initial stages of the experiment, Cynthia seems so chaste that Lysander is almost deceived back into belief. He has two rapturous soliloquies on his wife as a 'miracle of Nature'.[6] However, he does continue to press her, without ever explaining why he feels impelled to do so; and, once the first signs of weakness are detected in his wife, his is a truly Jacobean inquisitiveness. The following is his response to the discovery that his wife, on the second day, is not quite so firm as on the first:

> LYSANDER [*aside*] What's here! The maid hath certainly
>   prevail'd with her; methinks those clouds that
>   last night covered her looks are now dispers'd.
>   I'll try this further. – Save you, lady.
>
> (IV.iii.38–41)

The giveaway phrase is 'I'll try this further'. The words, 'try' or 'venture' typify the experimenter's determination to set aside normal scruple or the restraints of common caution, and push some project to its conclusion. Vindice, in *The Revenger's Tragedy*, is given an almost identical speech when he tries to corrupt his mother. First, in aside, the disguised and disconcerted experimenter betrays his fear that something morally dreadful is about to happen. Then, there is the determination nevertheless to proceed. Finally, he steps back into disguise, and briskly breaks back into normal dialogue. In both cases, the worst does happen; but the response of both men reveals an ingredient of excitement in the horror they express. Lysander seems almost intoxicated with the extravagance of the reversal he has just produced:

> O ye gods, In the height of her mourning,
> in a tomb, within sight of so many deaths, her
> husband's believ'd body in her eye, he dead a few
> days before! This mirror of nuptial chastity,

this votress of widow-constancy, to change her
faith, exchange kisses, embraces, with a stranger,
and, but my shame withstood, to give the utmost
earnest of her love to an eightpenny sentinel; in
effect, to prostitute herself on her husband's
coffin! Lust, impiety, hell, womanhood itself,
add, if you can, one step to this!

(V.i.115–23)

It is a speech which simply goes on too long to be merely one of
horror; and it develops in ways which are inconsistent with horror.
It is an exercise in expressing an idea, and therefore in a sense it
comes to play with the idea. The three components of the outrageous situation – the presence of the dead body, the apparent virtue
of the widow, the despicable status of the suitor – are all pushed
to their extreme. At the end, Lysander caps off his tirade by triumphantly finding a conclusive formula – 'to prostitute herself over
her husband's coffin' – for her guilt. The final sentence sounds
almost like a challenge. In rhythm and tone, the whole speech
sounds unexpectedly like the incredulous scoffs of Richard III, after
he has wooed the Lady Anne over the coffin of the husband he
has murdered.

The parallel seems particularly apt, since the murder of a husband
is precisely what Lysander is about to claim. This in itself marks
him off from the mere position of outraged husband. There is no
question as yet of him simply confronting Cynthia with the truth.
He must first discover exactly how far she can be pushed into
degradation. He must see how far he can go. Overhearing that a
corpse is missing from the graveyard, and knowing that the penalty
for graveyard custodians losing corpses is death, he returns to the
tomb and explains his predicament to Cynthia. The ensuing conversation is rich in the extravagant reversals that Jacobean drama
delights in, in its quest to prove the unreality of even the closest ties:

CYNTHIA   O this affright
          Torments me ten parts more than the sad loss
          Of my dear husband.
    LYSANDER [*aside*]. Damnation! – I believe thee.
    CYNTHIA   Yet hear a woman's wit;
          Take counsel of necessity and it.

I have a body here which once I lov'd
And honor'd above all, but that time's past –
LYSANDER [*aside*]. It is; revenge it, heaven.
CYNTHIA   – That shall supply at so extreme a need
The vacant gibbet.
LYSANDER   Cancro! What, thy husband's body?
CYNTHIA   What hurt is't, being dead, if't save the living?
LYSANDER O heart, hold in, check thy rebellious motion!
CYNTHIA   Vex not thyself, dear love, nor use delay.
Tempt not this danger; set thy hands to work.
LYSANDER I cannot do't; my heart will not permit
My hands to execute a second murder.
The truth is, I am he that slew thy husband.
CYNTHIA   The gods forbid!
LYSANDER It was this hand that bath'd my reeking sword
In his life blood, while he cried out for mercy.
But I, remorseless, paunch'd him, cut his throat,
He with his last breath crying, 'Cynthia!'
CYNTHIA   O thou hast told me news that cleaves my heart.
Would I had never seen thee, or heard sooner
This bloody story. Yet see, note my truth;
Yet I must love thee.
LYSANDER   Out upon thee, monster!
Go, tell the Governor. Let me be brought
To die for that most famous villainy,
Not for this miching base transgression
Of truant negligence.
CYNTHIA   I cannot do't.
Love must salve thy murder. I'll be judge
Of thee, dear love, and these shall be thy pains,
Instead of iron to suffer these soft chains.
                                    [*Embracing him*]
LYSANDER O, I am infinitely oblig'd.

(V.i.166–99)

Chapman's handling of role-playing here is highly intriguing. As
the experiment leads in increasingly appalling directions, Lysander
twice looks as if he is about to drop the pretence, break down, and
either weep or rage. He drops the 'aside'. He cries openly, 'O heart,
hold in'. He exclaims, 'I cannot do't'. However, what he 'cannot

do' is not what we expect. We anticipate, surely, a declaration that he cannot keep up the fiction. What he actually says – still very much in his role – is that he cannot use the corpse, because he was the murderer. Instead of stopping the game, he has pushed it a stage further. Again, the motive is surely to see if even this monstrous twist can find a limit to his wife's infamy. When, once again, she proves the contrary, it again looks as if he is about to simply break down: 'Out upon thee, monster'. Once more, however, the appearance deceives, and the experiment proceeds. He offers her the chance to have him executed for her husband's murder. Instead, she embraces him. Later, she consents to dragging the corpse to the gibbet in a noose.

Again, throughout the scene, there is a push towards extremes. In this last phase of it, Lysander creates the fullest possible contrasts. On the one hand is the defenceless loving husband, his wife's name on his dying lips. On the other is the remorseless butcher who disembowels him and cuts his throat. In doing so, he confronts Cynthia with the most lurid possible versions of her past and present sexual partners. It is not clear exactly what he wants to achieve. He seems by now unlikely to find a limit to his wife's iniquity, so presumably it is his intention simply to expose her to the maximum; to 'put wom[an] to the test' (V.i.222) to the fullest extent. Admittedly, he finally admits that he has had quite enough of experimentation: 'Thou foolish thirster after idle secrets/ And ills abroad, look home, and store, and choke thee' (227–8); he now plans, not further tests, but exposure. However, this happens only after the impulse to explore has run its full course and been exhausted, and this is the measure of how thoroughly Lysander has 'caught' and indeed exceeded the taint of his brother Tharsalio.

Tharsalio is established by Chapman, with a significant parallel plot, as a self-serving cynic. It is his mission to woo the wealthy widow, Countess Eudora, who has loudly proclaimed 'her open and often detestations of that incestuous life (as she term'd it) of widows' marriages, as being but a kind of lawful adultery' (II.iv.24–6). Like all cynics, he is convinced that all humanity has a breaking-point; it is merely a question of finding a way to penetrate the sham. The first approach – sheer boldness – is a failure. The second, implanting in the Duchess' mind the idea of his extraordinary sexual prowess, is a resounding success. With two paragons of women seduced within a single play, faith in chastity must emerge as credulity. Tharsalio continually plays with such terms:

THARSALIO

Tush, sister; suppose you should protest with solemn
oath (as perhaps you have done), if ever heaven hears your
prayers that you may live to see my brother nobly interred,
to feed only upon fish, and not endure the touch of flesh
during the wretched Lent of your miserable life; would you
believe it, brother?

LYSANDER

I am therein most confident

THARSALIO

Indeed, you had better believe it than try it. But pray,
sister, tell me – you are a woman – do not you wives nod
your heads and smile upon one another when ye meet
abroad?

CYNTHIA

Smile? Why so?

THARSALIO

As who should say, "Are not we mad wenches, that can lead
our blind husbands thus by the noses?" Do you not brag
amongst yourselves how grossly you abuse their honest
credulities? How they adore you for saints, and you believe
it, while you adhorn their temples, and they believe it not?
How you vow widowhood in their lifetime, and they believe
you, while even in the sight of their breathless corse, ere
they be fully cold, you enjoin embraces with his groom, or his
physician, and perhaps his poisoner; or at the least, by the
next moon (if you can expect so long) solemnly plight new
hymeneal bonds with a wild, confident, untamed ruffian?

(I.i.88–110)

These are prophetic words, since the 'widow' Cynthia will indeed
open her doors to a ruffian, who claims to be her husband's murderer. More to the point, here is the language of faith, credulity
and trial.

Tharsalio has travelled in Italy, and come back 'stuff'd. . . . . With
damn'd opinions and unhallowed thoughts/ Of womanhood, of all
humanity,/ Nay, deity itself' (II.i.47–50). He believes nothing sacred,
is convinced no one is faithful, and treats belief as gullibility; though
occasionally he mockingly urges Lysander, in the vein of Chaucer's
Miller, that foolish belief is far better than destructive curiosity. His

immediate motive for the provocation of Lysander is purely spiteful, a retaliation for Lysander's enjoyment of his (Tharsalio's) initial failure with Eudora. He simply wants to shake Lysander's complacency a little. However, when he succeeds so well, he allows things to proceed for a more calculating reason: Lysander is so besotted with Cynthia that he has willed all his money directly to her; so that if and when she remarried, the whole family might be impoverished. For this reason, even though he loves his 'sister well and must acknowledge her more than ordinary virtues' (II.iii.72–3), he is prepared to provoke Lysander into having to prove himself on this specific issue: the issue of the fidelity of a widow. If, after all, Lysander devised an experiment and found his 'widow' lacking, he must surely change his will. Tharsalio therefore urges the idea of a limited experiment, or rather of a 'trial' (a term respectable in romantic fiction); and the word, first used in II.i, is taken up four times in II.iii, and twice more in III.i. Later, the term is switched in favour of a 'taste' [test], and a 'project'. The word 'experiment' is itself used once in II.i.31, and these latter terms give a sense of something distinctly 'scientific' going on. Reinforcing this is a whole barrage of references to established sciences in relation to human behaviour. Tharsalio's own second attempt against Eudora is described by his accomplice as 'a villainous invention of thine, and had a swift operation; it took like sulphur' (II.iii.16–17). Lysander himself uses another chemical analogy about his wife: 'if she be gold she may abide the taste' (III.i.6). Tharsalio uses the language of alchemy when he urges how easy it is to 'boil [women's] appetites to a full height of lust and then take them down in the nick', or talks of their 'sublim'd spirits' (III.i.96–7, 103). Again, there is talk of metal in relation to the idea of trial later in the same scene (170–2), and there are scattered references to medicine or its 'faculty', and one reference to Ptolemy. At the end of this period of persuasion and preparation, Lysander is so fired with the idea of an experiment that, even though he deeply suspects his brother's motives, he will believe neither in his wife's innocence nor her guilt. He will 'believe nothing but what trial enforces' (III.i.180). In the end, it is an elementary enough chemical (alcohol) which produces the change and which breaks down moral resistance and heroic resolve. Ero the maid is the first to 'try' it, and wonders, since its effect is so remarkable, if the soldier has 'been a pothecary' (IV.ii.137). It has a similar loosening effect on Cynthia, and from that point onward she is transformed; so confirming Lysander's final conclusion: 'As men like this, let them try their wives again. Put women to the test; discover them' (V.i.221–3). Ironically, it is the instigator and designer of the experiment, Tharsalio, who at one stage has begun to doubt a result; hoping that 'our too curious trial hath not dwelt/ Too long on this unnecessary haunt'. A moment later, and he has seen Cynthia with the soldier; few successful experiments can have produced an ecstasy like his:

> She, she, she, and none but she.   *He dances and sings*
> She, only queen of love and chastity;
> O chastity, this women be.

> (V.i.9–10, 31–3)

The date of the tragedy, *Bussy D'Ambois* is uncertain, but the strongest evidence seems to place it in 1604, right at the inception of the drama of moral experiment. Yet it is usually described as a heroic play, and contains neither of the major indicators of the pioneers of the form; having no major discovery of moral frailty in a 'pure' character, nor any overt attempt to violate moral limits. At the same time, it does in some minor respects seem to work in ways which are detectably parallel to purer versions of morally experimental drama, and those parallels may help to make a play which was enormously popular then more comprehensible to us now.

The perennial problems that the play poses to modern readers are basically two fold. The first is the flimsiness of the action. Bussy says he rejects the court, but is tempted to try to rise there. He fights with and kills some haughty sneerers (offstage). He seduces someone else's wife, which earns him the enmity of her husband (Montsurry). He seems to hit it off with the king, which earns him the enmity of his original sponsor at court (Monsieur). His enemies ambush and murder him. This does not amount to much; and, even then, much of the action remains at the level of implication. We gather that the Monsieur had intended to use Bussy to assassinate the king, but we never see him attempt to persuade Bussy to that task. Next, Bussy seduces a woman who is no stranger to him, but one 'to whom [his] love hath long been vow'd in heart' (II.i.212). He tells us this in soliloquy; and his love, Tamyra, tells us, in a parallel soliloquy in the next scene, that she likewise loves Bussy. Both disclosures are complete surprises and have to be taken utterly on trust. We have no idea how or when this love came about, and we see almost nothing of it in action. The lovers appear together once, on the night of their first assignation. The topic of their conversation is the danger of the affair and the need for secrecy. They never meet again until the scene of Bussy's murder at the very end of the play, unless we count the scene where Bussy watches Tamyra in the conjuror's video-show. Thirdly, we see nothing of the process of Bussy's rise at court. We simply see King Henry enter, with Bussy as his established right-hand man, at the beginning of III.ii, inviting him to be his 'eagle' and to hawk at vice. So, three potential sources of genuine psychological action seem almost wilfully to be neglected by Chapman. In place of these possibilities, he instead steers his play into a series of 'flyting-matches', and courtship-games, which persist even into the fourth Act. It is fair to say that these verbal combats and their conventions are something of a lost language to a modern audience, but, until the intrigue drama leading to Bussy's assassination begins to dominate the last two Acts, it is all we have.

Then, there is the related problem of the character of Bussy himself. Almost every critic has sensed a major shortfall in the hero, between the very high valuation set on him by himself, by others in the play, and perhaps by his author, and the meagre evidence he gives us of his greatness. He is simply given very little to do which could prove it. What we see is difficult to distinguish from the actions of a posturing, ruffianly boor. He seems capable of no very persuasive proof of the ethical consistency or purity he claims. Initially all in favour of a retired life, despising greatness, he is rapidly persuaded (apparently by the prospect of Monsieur's gold, which he almost openly begs by his talk of the poverty of virtue) to 'rise in court' (I.i.130). Later, Tamyra's fear that 'he I love will loathe me when he sees/ I fly my sex, virtue, my renown/ To run so madly on a man unknown' (II.ii.124-6) turns out to be quite needless, since Bussy sees no moral paradox at all in the decision to seduce a woman because she is virtuous. His somewhat rough and ready morality here is conveniently endorsed by the Friar, his spiritual adviser and pander, whose cynical doctrine that, since coyness is an incorrigible 'frailty' in women (185), the first sexual approach should masquerade as something else, Bussy readily puts into action. When Bussy and Tamyra become lovers, Bussy dismisses her nervousness by telling her that 'sin is a coward, madam', but 'our ignorance tames us that we let/ His shadows fright us' (III.i.20, 22-3). The doctrine sounds remarkably similar to Richard

III's, 'Conscience is but a word that cowards use,/ Devis'd at first to keep the strong in awe'. The Machiavellian reverberations seem very much at odds with Bussy's continual insistence on his own virtue, and when, later on, he vows to 'sooth [Monsieur's] plots and strow my hate with smiles', he seems about to become a villain in earnest.

If, however, we can view Bussy as possessing at least some of the peculiarities of the moral experimenter, the ethical inconsistencies become less troublesome, and the problem of the flimsiness of the action also disappears.

Actually, right at the start, when he determines on trying his hand at court after all, he adopts two features which later become the stock-in-trade of figures such as Vindice, or Flamineo, or Bosola. Firstly, he is poor, and, despite protestations to the contrary, resents it. Secondly, he uses the language of experiment. One of the commonest words of that vocabulary is the verb, 'venture'. It made its initial appearance in the language in the later Middle Ages, but underwent an enormous expansion of use in the mid-sixteenth century, meeting the need of a word to express the spirit of daring risk in the hope of achievement. The heroes of the new-wave Jacobean tragedies, however, come to use the word in the specific and unprecedented context of compulsive spiritual risk in the hope of knowledge. Here, in the first scene, Bussy at first mocks the metaphoric merchant venturer who needs the humble home-bound knowledge of virtue to get safely into port. Fairly soon, however, deciding to surrender himself to the upward turn of fortune's wheel, but pondering also the old saw that '"Man's first rise is first step to his fall"', he decides to become an explorer himself: 'I'll venture that' (141–2). Another venture is to 'make/ Attempt of [Tamyra's] perfection' (II.ii.215–16). From the point of this decision onward, he consistently 'pushes his luck', and this actually helps to explain the apparent inertia of the plot, and the concentration on dialogues of insult. Bussy simply decides to expose himself to risk, to see what will happen. It is not his mission, in that case, genuinely to initiate the great actions which Monsieur suggests are within his grasp. Rather, what he must do is to provoke others, and wait for them to attack him. After practising on the underling, Maffe, whom he assaults, he moves briskly on to insult one of the most powerful men in the land, Guise, by pretending to court his wife, and to 'try'[7] a quarrel with 'the famous soldiers Barrisor,/ L'Anou, and Pyrhot, great in deeds of arms' (another somewhat arbitrary piece of information), which ends in their deaths. Pardoned for this, he then makes two more powerful enemies, by a calculated and insulting rejection of his sponsor, Monsieur, and the seduction of the wife of Montsurry. Informed by the ghost of the now-dead Friar of their plot on his life, he nevertheless insists on walking into the ambush in Tamyra's chamber. His professed reason for doing so is that the Friar's ghost is a fraud, yet he evidently still expects to be set upon as soon as he enters the room. Seen in this light, Bussy seems less concerned with maintaining the greatness or independence of his soul, than with exploring the limits of violence. His own metaphoric self-judgement, in his final words, is that he has 'like a falling star/ Silently glanc'd that, like a thunderbolt,/ Look'd to have stuck and shook the firmament' (V.iv.143–5), so defining his whole endeavour in life in terms of violent impact. This goes some way towards eliminating an otherwise disturbing or deliberately ironic conflict between lofty ethical ideals and unworthy or immoral actions. We must still seek the reason for his venture into violence, but it may be one which releases us from the assumption that his true motives lie in any kind of moral cause.

A clue to Bussy's reasons for what seems a bizarre course of action might be found in the play's persistent theme of fate, and the very consistent cluster of images used to explore the relationship between fate, prominence, and integrity. 'Fortune' is the first word of the play, and is seen as a force which exerts itself on 'great' men like a wind blowing on trees. The trees are alternately seen as whole or hollow. Great men are also seen as statues, alternately of solid marble or filled with debris. Bussy, in his first speech in the play, regards great men as trees troubled by winds, and as rubble-centred statues. Guise, in Act V, sees Bussy as a perfect but headless statue (V.iii.25–8). Monsieur, on the other hand, in the same scene sees Bussy as a solid tree which the wind will tear up, unlike the hollow men who will survive the blast (37–45). Two scenes later, Tamyra gives us a very similar metaphor, but her image of Bussy is as a tree without roots (12–13). Finally, in Bussy's death-speech, he hauls himself to his feet, determined to die 'like a Roman statue'. However, he does not claim to *be* of marble, but only that death will *make* him marble, as if with some kind of surface finish. These images seem to leave Bussy's ethical integrity in dispute, but establish that any man of prominence – moral or immoral – is exposed to destruction by fortune. The play's resemblance to the ancient form of the *de casibus* tragedy has often been noted. Bussy takes a conscious decision to step on to the 'deep nick in Time's restless wheel' (I.i.134) – actually *Fortune's* wheel – and immediately commits himself to the wheel's whole revolution. What is not so commonly noted is that he is challenging its power, exposing himself to the wind, and then taking every means to ensure that it blows hard. In the end, as R. J. Lordi observes, he succeeds in greatly accelerating the cycle of rise and fall.[8] It is the sole influence he actually achieves over his fortune. That does not alter the fact that it is his aim to tamper and experiment to the outer limits of his power.[9]

It is a play where many are interested in what their power can accomplish. Quite apart from the interest in political power, there is the Friar's sense of what is and is not possible as magician and as ghost – 'my power is limited; alas! I cannot' (V.iv.20); there is Bussy's own fascinated use of the ability he is granted to raise the spirit to which the Friar introduced him (V.iii.26); and even the spirit's own sense of his limited potency against that of other spirits (IV.ii.92–6). Bussy is viewed by Monsieur as an incubus whom he has raised, without the precaution of confining it within a circle: and therefore of unpredictable force (III.ii.358–61). It is a power which Bussy tries to exert over the very vocabulary of what defines him. He will acknowledge the verb 'to murder' in its active form, but professes not to understand 'to be murdered': it must be a word devised to fit lesser men (V.iv.22–31). He exerts a similar tyranny over moral concepts, telling Tamyra and his hidden murderers that he is a bulwark to Tamyra's integrity, and will 'project/ A life to her renown' (V.iv.59–60). Of course, he loses. He is murdered, and Tamyra does become a moral outcast. Bussy is forced back on the same defeatism he started with. Man, he tells us in his first speech is 'a dream/ But of a shadow'. At the end of his rise and fall, he tries to will his spirit not to follow the blood out of his body (V.iv.78–9); and, failing, concludes that all matter, even when abstracted or condensed, is 'a dream but of a shade' (86). Fate is the winner. He has described himself as being 'buckl'd in [his] fate' (39). What he meant is that Fate was his armour against his enemies. Ironically, the phrase also means that he is strapped to fortune's wheel. However, his whole endeavour had been to expose himself to her machinery, dare her, and see what happened.

Interestingly, there is a fair amount of the vocabulary of enquiry in the play, from the mouths even of Bussy's enemies. It becomes quite prominent from the appearance of the spirit Behemoth in IV.ii, who announces himself as 'emperor/ Of that inscrutable darkness where are hid/ All deepest truths and secrets never seen,/ All which I know, and command legions/ Of knowing spirits' (67–71). The names of the spirits are at worst those of pagan deities (Astorath), and the Friar summons them by his 'learned holiness' (45), but he nevertheless refers to Behemoth as 'great Prince of Darkness', and this seems to establish the act of enquiry as satanic. Later, the Friar tells Montsurry, who wants to find out the name of his wife's lover, 'It is a damn'd work to pursue those secrets/ That would ope more sin and prove springs of slaughter;/ Nor is't a path for Christian feet to tread,/ But out of all way to the health of souls' (V.i.30–4). Nevertheless, Montsurry and the other enemies of D'Ambois are undeterred. Seeking to 'prove'[10] Tamyra a whore, Montsurry puts her on the rack. Monsieur, preparing the ambush for Bussy, sees it as a kind of demonstration and proof of a proposition about Nature's merely material operation:

> Now shall we see that Nature hath no end
> In her great works responsive to their worths . . .
> And as illiterate men say Latin prayers
> By rote of heart and daily iteration,
> Not knowing what they say, so Nature lays
> A deal of stuff together, and by use,
> Or by the mere necessity of matter,
> Ends such a work, fills it, or leaves it empty
> Of strength or virtue, error or clear truth,
> Not knowing what she does.
>
> (V.ii.1–12)

'Yet you shall see it here', he says, thinking of how the great Bussy is about to be casually destroyed as he was pointlessly made. Bussy himself seems to know that he is in search of forbidden knowledge when he, too, summons Behemoth: 'I long to know . . . and be informed', he says, but his appeal is to the 'King of Flames' who 'hurl[s] instructive fire about the world' (V.iii.32–3, 41, 44). It is an interesting array of beliefs. Nature exists, but is a blind force, operating by chance collision of matter, rather than by design. Fortune exists, as a mechanism operating by its laws of revolution. The powers of darkness exist, and are the holders of all the secrets of the physical laws. The Christian God, however, seems a notable absentee from the scene; except perhaps to witness to earth's degraded state. 'Now is it true', says Montsurry, accepting Copernicus along with his wife's infidelity, 'earth moves, and heaven stands still' (V.i.161). With that revolution, she turns her hypocritical face away from heaven, and reveals, instead, her posterior. Yet, he still wants to find out more horrors: 'I'll after/ To see what guilty light gives this cave eyes,/ And to the world sing new impieties' (191–3). Clearly, Chapman was interested in the impulse of moral experiment, and, though his clearest attempts in it are in his comedies, it is pleasing to find also such unmistakable evidence of it in his most famous tragedy.

2

Disguised Dukes:
The Malcontent, and *Measure for Measure*

The idea of the 'disguised duke' was one of the more useful resources of the morally experimental dramatist. Intriguingly, the plays which use the motif sometimes also include a chastity test, and, like the chastity test, the disguised duke device permits the protagonist the role of fascinated observer and participant in a situation wherein even his virtuous subjects are exposed to risk. The plot usually involves a Duke who is either an absentee, or is deposed. He returns to his own kingdom in disguise, watches, participates, and inevitably manipulates. A character, therefore, who is accustomed to the forthright exercise of rightful power, inevitably finds himself transformed into something more underhand. The disguise which he is impelled to adopt may become a kind of temporary licence. The upright ruler may escape the responsibilities of power and accept the opportunity to dabble and to tamper. In such a case, the disguised duke may seem not dissimilar from the full blown experimenters of Jacobean tragedy, whose entire quest is to destroy the reality and solidity of stable identity and stable ties.[1]

Marston's Altofronto is a deposed duke, disguised as a 'malcontent'[2] and intent on recovering his dukedom. While remaining viruous in his own eyes, he nevertheless acts in ways remote from his own former identity. Conversely, Shakespeare's Duke sets up a deliberate experiment to test his subjects' virtue and find it lacking, but then for the rest of the play, in his very different disguise of Friar, attempts to retreat from the experiment and to sabotage its results. These 'disguised duke' tragicomedies are therefore both half-way houses in the drama of moral experiment. Certainly, like Chapman's comedies, both plays end up reaffirming or at least restoring the old order of things. Yet, the presence of experiment in the plays of two such conservative writers as Marston (a conservative at least in his own eyes) and Shakespeare, is another significant testimony to the infectiousness of the new impulse.

The beginning of Marston's tragi-comedy *The Malcontent* finds the rightful Duke, Altofronto, already disguised as the malcontent, Malevole. He had been deposed from the dukedom of Genoa by the puppet-duke Pietro who was placed in office by the Medici of Florence, to whom he was related by his marriage to Aurelia. It is Altofronto's aim to recover political power, though as yet the means are not clear. He has at least endeared himself to Pietro by his bluntness, and now plans further to win his favour by exposing Aurelia as an adulteress; this at least gives him the satisfaction of tormenting the usurper. In his hopes of regaining the dukedom he has a rival, however, in the ambitious villain Mendoza, named as successor by Pietro, and now plotting with Aurelia to murder him. It is – naturally – Malevole whom he approaches and bribes to do the deed. He also employs him to seduce his own (Altofronto's) imprisoned wife. Later, with Altofronto using a second disguise, Mendoza hires him to kill his first persona, Malevole.

The plot closely anticipates that of *The Revenger's Tragedy*, with the hero being employed, in malcontented disguises in both plays, to commit murder and to procure women who turn out to belong to his closest family. In the later play, Vindice does indeed commit murders. Altofronto/Malevole does not. Interestingly, though, he does undertake the other evil office that comes with the disguise, the procurement of his own wife for his duke-employer, just as Vindice in the later play does agree to try to procure his own sister. The enterprise demonstrates in the clearest terms the extent to which disguise entails moral compromise and indeed moral experiment. Whatever right and justice initially exists on the side of the protagonists of both plays, their revenges lure them into uncharted and dangerous moral territory.

Central to such experimentation is the idea of role-playing. Disguise serves as more than a convenient trick. It involves a definite loss of the habits, values, and restraints of one's normal identity. It frees the disguiser to do things which would be otherwise inconceivable, as he in a sense becomes what he poses as. In this way, a high-minded Duke can become a foul-mouthed cynic and a procurer. If he does not become a murderer, it is a difference of degree rather than of kind.

Malevole/Altofronto is the major figure through whom Marston explores his theme of role-playing. However, the play's interest in the theme is endemic. From the *Shrew*-like Induction, with actors appearing in their own persons to discuss the play with other actors disguised as spectators, to the stock device of the concluding masque-within-the-play, *The Malcontent* demonstrates its interest in acting and illusion. Disguise is prolific, and role-playing even more so, even by those not otherwise disguised. Take, for instance, the passage in which the ambitious villain Mendoza rehearses the usurping duke Pietro in the scenario for the murder of one Ferneze. Ferneze has been sleeping with Pietro's wife, Aurelia. So too has Mendoza, who devises this murder both to eliminate a rival lover, and to make a steady political ally of Aurelia in his own plans to capture the dukedom. The passage seems very like a director's first instructions about a scene:

> Ferneze flies – let him; to me he comes; he's kill'd
> By me – observe, by me. You follow; I rail,
> And seem to save the body. Duchess comes,
> . . . I storm,
> I praise, excuse Ferneze, and still maintain
> The Duchess' honor; she for this loves me.
> I honor you, shall know her soul, you mine.
>
> (I.vii.56–64)

The entrances, the railing or storming, are all envisaged as an extravagantly-acted part. Elsewhere, the theme of acting is sustained with constant verbal reminders: 'the scene grows full' (II.v.158); 'play I the free-breath'd discontent?' (I.iv.31); 'the rest of idle actors idly part' (V.vi.160).

However, this is more than merely the characters assuming identities to deceive others. The first people they deceive are themselves. They habitually conceive self-glorifying visions, and their public 'performances' merely isolate the most calculated moments in a process which is congenital.

When Mendoza considers his recent rise in court favour, the soliloquy typifies the way the court's panders, bawds and sycophants habitually recast their lives, in imagination, as heroism and romance. We see many public occasions at the court during the play, but never anything remotely approaching the grandeur of, for instance, Mendoza's reverie:

> To be a favorite, a minion. To have a
> general timorous respect observe a man, a stateful silence

in his presence, solitariness in his absence, a confused hum
and busy murmur of obsequious suitors training him, the
cloth held up and way proclaimed before him, petitionary
vassals licking the pavement with their slavish knees whilst
some odd palace-lamprels that engender with snakes, and
are full of eyes on both sides, with a kind of insinuated
humbleness fix all their delights upon his brow! O blessed
state! What a ravishing prospect doth the Olympus of
favor yield!

(I.v.23–33)

Even in a private speech such as this one, Mendoza's imagination
works along theatrical lines. We are listening to a scene being
'blocked'. He presents us with a detailed *mise-en-scène*, its extras
carefully deployed, and its sound-effects calculated. This is indeed
an Entrance, though the scene really has only one character. It is
difficult to tell whether the 'palace-lamprels that engender with
snakes' are a matter of costume or of metaphor, but either way,
Mendoza dehumanizes his supernumaries so as to enhance himself.
His admirers are an anonymous mob, mute except for their 'confused hum' of respect, and animated only by his presence. These
delusions of grandeur are most marked in a passage four scenes
later, when, having narrowly escaped detection by Pietro as one
of Aurelia's lovers, he renews his determination to break all natural
laws, rather than lose power:

Shall I, whose very 'Hum' struck all heads bare,
Whose face made silence, creaking of whose shoe
Forc'd the most private passages fly ope,
Scrape like a servile dog at some latch'd door?

(II.i.18–21)

The removal of any intervening agency between his merest gesture
and the surrender of all things to his will indicates the extent to
which he regards his own powers as magical.

On a comically reduced level, the same addiction to day-dream
is found in such minor characters as Bilioso, as when he envisages
how he will bear himself on his diplomatic mission to Florence: he
will be,

Proud enough, and 'twill do well enough. As I walk up and down the chamber, I'll spit frowns about me, have a strong perfume in my jerkin, let my beard grow to make me look terrible, salute no man beneath the fourth button; and 'twill do excellent.

(III.i.104–8)

Elsewhere, this Ur-Knight of the Burning Pestle claims that,

I have measured calves with most of the palace, and they come nothing near me; besides, I think there be not many armors in the arsenal will fit me, especially for the headpiece . . . I can eat stew'd broth as it comes seething off the fire, or a custard as it comes reeking out of the oven; and I think there are not many lords can do it.

(V.i.8–15)

Though obviously burlesque, these passages maintain Marston's idea that the Genoese court habitually constructs heroic versions of itself, no matter how meagre the raw material. The role-playing ends only when the end of the play terminates the period of license. Mendoza's amazed questions, 'Are we surpris'd? What strange delusions mock/ Our senses? Do I dream? or Have I dreamt/ This two days' space?' mark the end of a trance. He actually says, 'Where am I?' (V.vi.112–14).

The 'dreams' of Genoa had been detected by Malevole very early in the play:

here is a pander jewel'd; there is a fellow in shift of satin this day that could not shift a shirt t'other night. Here a Paris supports that Helen; there's a Lady Guinevere bears up that Sir Lancelot. Dreams, dreams, visions, fantasies, chimeras, imaginations, tricks, conceits!

(I.iii.50–5)

The passage draws attention to classical and romance allusion, both of which are prevalent in the play and are usually regarded as didactic in intention. Bernard Harris in the Introduction to his New Mermaids edition believes that most of the references are 'associated with the theme of adultery, and are thereby related to the theme . . . of usurpation, and its attendant topics of treachery and inconstancy'. The account is plausible, but a non-didactic interpretation may equally be possible. Indisputably, Genoa's conscience is chaotic. Guilt and innocence collide with a frequently comic incongruity:

> Beware an hypocrite;
> A churchman once corrupted, O avoid!
> > *Shoots under his belly.*
> A fellow that makes religion his stalking-horse,
> He breeds a plague. Thou shalt poison him.

> (IV.iii.120–3)

Yet, the way in which the same character, Mendoza, uses classical allusion does not merely indicate an unconscious appeal to standards which condemn him. Mendoza calls on ancient mythology for material to sustain his fantasies:

> He that attempts a princess' lawless love
> Must have broad hands, close heart, with Argus' eyes,
> And back of Hercules, or else he dies.

> (II.v.6–8)

He has just stabbed Ferneze, his rival, and evidently his inferior. To survive, the successful suitor must be, like himself, of heroic proportions. The classical figures are used to create a vaguely glamorous aura with which the speaker believes he accords, and this must have some bearing on our view of similar references by Malevole. When classical allusion, and quotations from Seneca are heard from the mouths of even minor characters, it cannot be ignorance which explains the apparent complacency with which they receive, for instance, Malevole's suggestion that Mendoza is, like Aegisthus, 'a filthy incontinent fleshmonger, such a one as thou art' (I.v.10–11); or that Bianca's husband, Bilioso, is a 'decayed Jason' (II.ii.18). It must be that even insulting analogies with classical figures are felt to be flattering. To be reminded that there are ancient precedents for one's meanest behaviour provides gratifying sanction for it. Such reminders tend actually to glamourize in its own eyes an impoverished society. Since the one possibility no character can entertain is of his own mediocrity, appeals to the classics provide a means of fictionalizing trivial affairs, to make them correspond with 'dreams, visions, fantasies'. When Mendoza views his poor expedients of Act One as the heroic defence of power by superhuman ruthlessness – 'Nothing so holy,/ No band of nature so strong . . ./ But I'll profane, burst, violate,/ 'Fore I'll endure disgrace' (II.i.13–17) – he supports the illusion with a quotation from *Thyestes* on the fall of greatness (26). Just as Maria, the virtuous wife of Altofronto feels her fortitude to be sustained by references to 'Cleopatra's asps, and Portia's coals' (V.iii.31), in no less potent a way, the repeated reminders to and by the corrupt characters of the examples of Hercules, or Ulysses, or Arthur, help to aggrandize their vices.

In all this, it is remarkable how little the satirist/railer is felt to present a dissenting voice. In, say, Webster, the case is entirely different. Faced with Ferdinand's ridiculous claim that 'He that can compass me, and know my drifts,/ May say he hath put a girdle 'bout the world/ And sounded all her quicksands', Bosola tells him roundly that 'you are/ Your own chronicle too much; and grossly/ Flatter yourself' (*The Duchess of Malfi*, III.i.84–9). Marston had a long record as a satirist, but his protagonist here seems to feel no such need to deflate self-esteem. When, at the end of a typically flippant speech, he calls Mendoza, 'good mischievous incarnate devil . . . Ah, you inhuman villain' (II.v.132–3), the apparently amiable exclamation can only serve to feed Mendoza's already high conceit of his own villainy. Malevole's surprising failure to contest the vanity of the Genoese court is most marked when he is employed by Mendoza to procure his own (Altofronto's) wife: a mission familiar in the drama of moral experiment. He fails, but not before he has exercised all his mocking salesmanship in presenting to her a version of the Genoese dream, this time using romance allusion rather than classical:

Mully, he that loves thee is a duke, Mendoza. He will maintain thee royally, love thee ardently, defend thee powerfully, marry thee sumptuously, and keep thee in despite of Rosiclere or Donzel del Phoebo. Here's jewels.

(V.iii.15–18)

Once again, Malevole adopts rather than contests the typical
inflated idiom, and, as with all moral experimenters, seems to
experience only the faintest of qualms at carrying out the commission to corrupt someone close to him. Actually, even that small
protest seems less a matter of balking against the immoral mission
itself, than of a weariness with the railing mode – '[*aside*] O God,
how loathsome this toying is to me! That a Duke should be forc'd
to fool it!' (41–2). In any case, the qualm is momentary: 'Well, better
play the fool lord than be that fool lord' (43–4). At no time, even
when speaking of it to his allies at the end of Act IV does he take
the time to express any kind of shock at his mission of seduction.
Nor should we expect any real distaste for Genoa's mode of thought.
Malevole's obvious control of the action may make Mendoza's conceit seem absurd, but at the same time the analogies in his commen-
tary on that action seem to give the self-esteem some warrant. P.
J. Finkelpearl must be wrong when, dealing with Malevole's
'dreams' speech, he says: 'Throughout the play, Malevole's goal is
to make people see the world as his 'dreams' have revealed it to
him'.[3] Actually, until he finally demolishes it, Malevole helps fantasy
to grow, The 'phantasmagorical impression' which Marston creates
through him depends on it, and as much as any other character
his imagination is excited by it. Warning Bilioso not to leave his
wife unprotected in his absence, he imagines for him all the perils
of a 'lady guardianless':

> incens'd with wanton sweets,
> Her veins fill'd high with heating delicates,
> Soft rest, sweet music, amorous masquerers,
> Lascivious banquets, sin itself gilt o'er,
> Strong fantasy tricking up strange delights,
> . . . Ulysses absent
> O Ithaca, can chastest Penelope hold out?

(III.ii.36–49)

The whole speech extends over 25 lines, and what is most evident
is the 'strong fantasy' not of Bilisoso, his wife, or her potential
suitors, but of Malevole himself. The passage vibrates with sensu-
ous excitement. Malevole may not indulge in daydreams on his
own account, but he is clearly stimulated by the fantasies he creates
for others. He is exercising the talents of a kind of licensed pornog-

rapher and publicist, providing an articulate voice for Genoese pruri-
ence. It is in vain that Webster, in his Induction for the play's Globe
performance, makes Burbage demand, 'shall we protest to the ladies
that their painting makes them angels? . . . No, sir, such vices . . .
should be cured as men heal tetters, by casting ink upon them'
(64–9). The promised reductiveness never materializes. Altofronto/
Malevole, like Mendoza and the rest of them, deals in hyperbole,
and it is difficult to insist on the mere triviality of what we see of
Genoa. Eugene Waith is nearer the truth with his remark that 'the
exaggerated evil of the court of Genoa is largely a feat of satirical
rhetoric'.[4] The satirist is responsible both for the attack and for
inflating the attractiveness of what he attacks.

Our problem is to decide how far all this is a deliberate tactical
manoeuvre by Altofronto in his disguise as Malevole – to lull his
enemies, for instance – or how far Altofronto may be identified
with his persona. Malevole's first meeting with his confidant, Celso,
in Act One, gives us important clues. As M. L. Wine says, in his
introduction to the Regents Renaissance Drama edition of the play,
'the scenes in which he can relax for a moment to confide in his
one friend, Celso, are scenes of relief in the play itself'.[5] Here, if
anywhere, we shall find the 'real' Altofronto:

> Why, man, we are all philosophical monarchs
> Or natural fools. Celso, the court's afire;
> The duchess' sheets will smoke for't ere it be long.
> Impure Mendoza, that sharp-nos'd lord, that made
> The cursed match link'd Genoa with Florence,
> Now broad-horns the duke, which he now knows.
> Discord to malcontents is very manna;
> When the ranks are burst, then scuffle, Altofront.

> (I.iv.32–9)

If Marston wishes to dissociate the Duke from the disguise, it is
remarkably careless of him to make him refer to himself as a Malcontent, and give him sentiments appropriate to the name. The speech
again demonstrates a fast-paced elation, a guerilla's delight in
exploitable chaos.[6] It contains also an interesting distortion of the
word, 'philosophical'. Like 'scholar' in the mouth of Mendoza, the
word means only 'machiavellian'. It is not the dignity of the scholar
and the statesman that here absorbs Altofronto's meditations, but

the prospect of a 'scuffle'. As Finkelpearl remarks, Altofronto is 'a true malcontent posing as a malcontent';[7] the disguise is a matter of language rather than of attitude. This is all that is meant by the stage direction, 'Bilioso *entering*, Malevole *shifteth his speech'*.

If more proof were needed than simply words, of Malevole's submergence in his role, his deeds seem to supply it. In fact, of the three Dukes of Genoa in this play (Altofronto/Malevole himself, Pietro who succeeds him, and the villain Mendoza), it seems to be the usurper Pietro who most clearly seems to qualify as an innocent moralist. In Altofronto's case, it was by innocence, by being 'suspectless, too suspectless' (I.iv.14), that he lost the throne. He is unlikely to repeat the mistake, and his rhetorical question, 'Who can sink who close can temporise?' (IV.v.142) fully matches the political realism of Mendoza's conviction that, 'Fortune still dotes on those who cannot blush' (II.i.29). The virtuous outsider is therefore not the rightful duke at all. It is Pietro who is the virtuous odd man out.

The best sign of that oddity is his complete neglect of role-playing. He welcomes Malevole for reasons very different from Mendoza's (who of course wishes only to use Malevole as a tool-villain):

> I like him;
> faith, he gives good intelligence to my spirit, makes me
> understand those weaknesses which others' flattery palliates.

> (I.ii.26–8)

This dedication to self-knowledge is the antithesis of the self-deluding fantasies of the rest of the court. It is not surprising that he is also quite incapable of acting a part. His emotional honesty makes this impossible. Where others can simulate or disguise emotions at will, Pietro can only express what he feels. Informed of Mendoza's adultery with his wife, Pietro has to confront him directly, expressing a spluttering moral indignation as unfeigned as it is exceptional: 'Thou, thou hast dishonoured my bed' (I.vii.5). His honesty makes him manipulable with ease, as Mendoza goes on to demonstrate.

It is true that Pietro does adopt the role of a friar in Act Four, who comes to Mendoza to announce Pietro's (i.e. his own) suicide because of his wife's infidelity. A. C. Kirsch believes that he contrives the performance as an outlet for his feelings.[8] In reality, though, the contrivance is Malevole's:

Come, shade thee with this disguise. If! Thou shalt
handle it; he shall thank thee for killing thyself. Come, follow my
directions, and thou shalt see strange sleights.

(III.v.26–8)

Malevole directs the whole performance, providing a framework
for Pietro's emotional outburst, for his own ends. As he knows,
Pietro is not really required to impersonate a friar. All he has to do
is to recount what 'Pietro' is supposed to have said before throwing
himself into the sea. This leaves him, in effect, speaking in his own
person; not acting at all, but giving vent to his very real personal
grief about his wife's betrayal. Malevole's idea of the disguise provides the quotation-marks which Pietro then fills with the
emotionalism which is his normal mode in the play:

> Methinks I hear him yet – "O female faith!
> Go sow the ingrateful sand, and love a woman . . ."

(IV.iii.25–48)

and so on, for another twenty lines.

The contrast with Malevole is stark. If Pietro cannot play the part
of a priest, Malevole can, as he shows in his conversion of Pietro
to a religious contempt of the world. The usurper's penitence is no
doubt wholesome in itself, but Malevole's motives for inducing it
are disingenuous. He works on Pietro's disillusionment so as to
produce in him a contempt which is specific: a contempt of
sovereignty:

> this earth is . . . the very muck hill on which the sublunary
> orbs cast their excrements. Man is the slime of this
> dung pit, and prices are the governors of these men; for,
> for our souls, they are as free as emperors, all of one
> piece; there goes but a pair if shears betwixt an emperor
> and the son of a bag-piper – only the dyeing, dressing,
> pressing, glossing makes the difference. Now, what art
> thou like to lose?

(IV.v.107–16)

We are alerted by this uncharacteristic scorn for the value of costume. Altofronto himself does not despise the dukedom. On the
contrary, all his efforts in the play, and here particularly, are directed
towards regaining an office on which he places the highest value.
He encourages Pietro to renounce the dukedom, only in order to
get closer to reclaiming it for himself. When he finally reveals his
identity to Pietro, and celebrates the reclaiming of the sinner, he
revealingly mixes piety with self-congratulation on the success of
a political manoeuvre:

> Who doubts of providence
> That sees this change? A hearty faith to all!
> He needs must rise, who can no lower fall
>
> (IV.v.136–40)

Typically, the final emphasis is on himself, and the speech recalls
several others in which the religiose rubs shoulders with the prag-
matic.[9] Even his final speech on the political theme, in which he
sums up the lessons learned, combines a tribute to 'heaven's impos'd
condition' with the reminder that 'th'inconstant people/ Love many
princes merely for their faces/ And outward shows' (V.iv.138–42).
We can feel confident that Altofronto will never again neglect the
ruler's need to promote fictions, and that Pietro will remain alone
in rejecting 'court-like shows' (IV.v.13). Altofronto shares none of
Mendoza's evil, but he shares his tactics, and only by 'virtuous
Machiavellianism'[10] is right upheld.

However, it is at least debatable whether the play concludes that
these tactics can now be laid aside, so that Altofronto can become
'himself' again. Everything we have seen of him indicates that the
local preference for myth and fiction becomes completely ingrained
in Altofronto. Yet, Marston plies us with a full-scale ritual at the
end of the play of a final discarding of disguise.

We can easily see in this play, in fact, the fault that dogs *Antonio's
Revenge* to a much larger extent. Marston, the 'gross-jawed' satirist,
who later takes holy orders, tends to become confused on issues
of righteousness. In *Antonio's Revenge*, there are the most glaring
inconsistencies between the professed piety of the avengers – the
hero in particular – and the brutality of their actions. The first step
in that revenge is Antonio's murder of his enemy's young son, Julio
(who incidentally seems greatly attached to Antonio). The hero

uses the traditional antinomy of body and soul, as he 'mangles' (his own word) the child's body:

> Thy father's blood that flows within thy veins
> Is it I loathe, is that revenge must suck.
> I love thy soul.
>
> (III.i.179–81)

Having tormented the villain Pietro himself at the end of the play by cutting out his tongue, showing him his son's body, rushing at him and pretending to stab him, before finally despatching him, Antonio exults at 'standing triumphant over Belzebub' (V.iii.138). If we expect a less naive view from his elder co-revenger, Pandulpho, we are disappointed. Like Altofronto, he comes to equate virtue squarely with violence: 'he that wants soul to kill a slave,/ Let him die slave and rot in peasant's grave' (V.ii.86–7). At the same time, he sees no incongruity in then retiring to monastic contemplation:

> We know the world; and did we know no more
> We would not live to know; but since constraint
> Of holy bands forceth us to keep this lodge
> Of dirt's corruption till dread power calls
> Our soul's appearance, we will live enclos'd
> In holy verge of some religious order.
>
> (V.iii.147–52)

Marston is highly unusual in sparing his revengers at the end of the play, and Michael Scott argues that we are meant to feel uneasy with the conclusion.[11] Yet Pandulpho's speech here implies that they are a kind of élite, in touch with 'more' than ordinary knowledge. Nothing but our own assumption that surely this must be ironic suggests that Marston's position is not identical with Pandulpho's. We are not only meant to separate the 'meanly-soul'd' Pietro from his great-souled enemies, but are supposed to continue to do so, even when their actions seem identical. We are urged not to baulk even at infanticide.

That scene is a particularly powerful scene of violence. Marston is especially skilful at imitating the electricity, the abruptness of actual brutality. We watch Antonio's mounting hysteria in this scene, from the 'punches' with which he obscenely rehearses the murder, to the multiple stabs of the murder itself, through to the mangling of the body. Yet, he then 'heaves [his] blood-dyed hands to heaven', and proclaims 'Sound peace and rest to church' (III.i.211, 214). At the end, after the murder of Pietro, the play turns to images of purgation. The band of grave senators (especially invented for the purpose) congratulates the killers on 'ridding huge pollution from the state' (V.iii.130). Antonio exclaims, 'First let's cleanse our hands,/ Purge hearts of hatred' (154–5). The naive cathartic assumptions match his delusion that, when he murders Pietro, he is 'all soul, all heart, all spirit' (V.iii.48).[12]

In *The Malcontent*, therefore, we can anticipate that Marston will wish us to accept Altofronto entirely on his own valuation. He may wish us to detect self-interest in Altofronto's part in Pietro's repentance, yet seems at the same time to wish us to view both the event and the agent with reverence. Alvin Kernan is quite right to detect an increased amount of reference to religion at the end of the play (the part of Altofronto's virtuous wife Maria is particularly useful for achieving this). Altofronto himself is increasingly made to assume the divinity which hedges his office. When Pietro makes his vows to heaven, it is Altofronto who receives them: 'Thy vows are heard, and we accept thy faith' (IV.v.129). On the overthrow of Mendoza, it is Altofronto again who blithely arbitrates the question of 'grace' (V.vi.121). Marston's intentions are clear enough. The problem is that the transformation of Malevole back into Altofronto is as unsatisfactory as the play's perfunctory and implausible comic ending. Yet, our sense of violation is perhaps the measure of how far Marston has surrendered to the temptations of moral experiment latent in the device of the disguised duke. Altofronto *became* Malevole, and as such he also became a part of what he was setting out to defeat.

Shakespeare's *Measure for Measure*, perhaps written in the same year, similarly tries to retreat from an experiment, but is initially an even clearer case of the disguised duke convention being used for morally experimental purposes (insofar as anything is clear in this ambiguous play). The sabbatical leave that Duke Vincentio takes from the dukedom of Vienna is obscure in motive. Part of his own account includes the confession that the laws have become slack and almost disused. He now wishes to enforce them rigorously, but is afraid to do so in his own person. Instead, he selects a deputy to delegate the unpopular task to, and to deflect the blame from himself. This is the motive he offers his confidant, the friar: the law has become like 'an overgrown lion in a cave,/ That goes not out to prey' (I.iii.22–3).

The reference is a curious one to apply to laws, as is also the later reference to the chosen deputy enforcing laws under the 'ambush of [Vincentio's] name', and there is also something slightly distasteful about the device of using another man to collect a blame that Vincentio has richly deserved by his inconsistent government. The idea of ambush would however fit a man of secretive character, and this seems to be the case. He professes to love 'the life remov'd' (8). Yet he proposes, not, as we might expect, to enjoy some months of monastic retirement while Angelo enforces the laws, but rather to remain in his dukedom in disguise, 'to behold [Angelo's] sway' (43). He apparently has a reason for doing so. As he tells Friar Thomas,

> Lord Angelo is precise;
> Stands at a guard with envy; scarce confesses
> That his blood flows, or that his appetite
> Is more to bread than stone; hence shall we see,
> If power change purpose, what our seemers be.
>
>   (50–4)

The remark is casual, but it suggests a second motive for his plot, which may indeed be just as potent as the professed primary one of the strict enforcement of law. The whole tenor of Vincentio's remarks about Angelo indicate his doubts whether Angelo's strict virtue is not altogether too good to be true. In the light of his doubts, and particularly in the light of Vincentio's insistence on watching what happens, it is impossible not to treat the entire leave-of-absence ploy as Vincentio's experiment on Angelo's virtue: to discover either that his virtue is a fraud, and the true self will be revealed, or that his virtue is real, but that power will corrupt it. Again, the tone of Vincentio's comments strongly suggests his expectation that one of these things will happen.

Actually, there is interesting testimony later in the play that it was only the first of these possibilities that interested the Duke. That testimony again comes from the Duke himself, at the point in the play where he invents the idea of the bed-trick. This device depends entirely on the availability of a suitable bed-substitute for

Isabella: preferably, one with whom there is no sin involved in sleeping with Angelo. That suitable woman is available: Mariana, Angelo's former fiancée. To repudiate her, when her dowry was lost at sea, Angelo even slandered her, 'pretending in her discoveries of dishonour' (III.i.227).

At this point, however, Vincentio's defenders urge us not to deduce that the Duke knew about Angelo all along. Mariana is a spur-of-the-moment invention, the mere objective correlative of a plot device. We should make no connection between this revelation which involves retrospectively changing Angelo's character, and Vincentio's knowledge of that character at the beginning of the play.

If this be so, it seems careless to have re-used the key word about Angelo: the word which would immediately invite connections to be made. The Duke does so, when he describes Angelo as 'well-seeming'. It is altogether too much to ask, to deny this obvious verbal connection, and its implication that Vincentio did indeed know right from the beginning just what the 'seemer' Angelo was. This in itself raises interesting questions about Vincentio's responsibilities as Duke. If his true motive for using a temporary deputy were to resurrect strict moral laws, how odd it was to put the task in the hands of a man known to be unscrupulous. If on the other hand his true motive was to test a man he knows to be unscrupulous, how odd it was to risk the well-being of his subjects in the process.

Perhaps a still more troubling question is why he should wish to test a man already known to be hollow. The answer would have to be that, like all other experimenters in Jacobean drama, he actually wants to discover moral limits and breaking points, and also wants to see those moral limits broken. He already knows Angelo's willingness to leave a lady destitute and then, to save his own reputation, also rob her of the one thing she had left: her good name. For most people, that knowledge would be all that was necessary. However, the Duke wants stronger proof of Angelo's worthlessness, wants him to commit some outrage, wants to see him break moral limits. He puts him in the ideal position for these things to happen. It is still a disturbing gamble with the safety of his own people, but the very chances it takes seem to argue beyond doubt how clinical is Angelo's interest in the affair.[13] Indeed, his early words about his people argue his dispassionateness. He 'loves' them, but does 'not like to stage [him] to their eyes./ Though it do well, [he does] not relish well/ Their loud applause and aves vehement'. Later on he speaks slightingly of the story about his journey to Poland which he has 'strewed . . . in the common ear'. He loves remoteness, and has always 'held in idle price to haunt assemblies/ Where youth and cost, witless bravery keeps'.[14] So strong is this vein of distaste in the early speeches that it is hard to believe in Vincentio's fourteen-year failure to enforce the available moral laws. Conversely, his evident distaste for ordinary people and ordinary pleasures makes it easier to understand his willingness to put them at risk. The dukedom becomes a kind of chemist's retort, into which he stirs ingredients he knows to be volatile. It therefore is apt that, at the end of the play, he should declare, 'I have seen corruption boil and bubble/ Til it o'errun the stew' (V.i.316–17) – the word 'stew' is usually interpreted as meaning some kind of cauldron – and odd only that he should seem to complain about it. The chemical reaction was of his own making.

As the plot develops, the Duke begins not merely to observe the action but to dabble in it. His first action is simply to play his part, as friar, in his two interviews with the condemned man Claudio and his pregnant fiancée Juliet.[15] Later, of course, there are the faintly ludicrous plot manipulations of beds and beheadings, in which he scrambles to retain control of events. Then there is the final phase, in which he engineers forgiveness by pretending to represent the harshest 'justice'. The movement is towards progressively heavier involvement in the action, until, unmasking himself for the final phase, the Duke occupies a point of absolute centrality and overt direction of the entire outcome. The plot of *Promos and Cassandra* which Shakespeare inherited as the basis for his story necessitates the second of these two phases. Shakespeare's own theme of forgiveness and mercy demands the third phase. The first can be explained as the first step towards the Duke's final emergence as a 'power divine' (V.i.367) supplanting strict justice with grace.

Yet, whatever the special pleading on the score of the play's theme or sources, it is unrealistic to try to pretend that the Duke is not really a character at all, but only a symbol of grace.[16] He is on stage, he does have a character, and what he says inevitably has some effect on how we view that character.

The first implication which is difficult to avoid is that a Duke, who so systematically intervenes in an action, may be by temperament a manipulator. The well-meaning cynic, Lucio, whom Shakespeare so entertainingly twice thrusts into the disguised Duke's company in Act IV to slander him, has interesting testimony to this effect, when he repeatedly refers to the Duke's furtiveness and in particular describes him as 'the old fantastical Duke of dark corners' (IV.iii.156). Lucio is clearly initially introduced in order to help lighten the play's tone to something more consistent with a comic outcome. His effect, though, is inevitably to diminish the Duke, both by slinging mud which sticks, and by so clearly irritating him. Lucio, in brief, makes the theory of the Duke as 'power divine' rather hard to swallow.

The sheer quantity of intervention which is needed is a further complication of our view of him. So frequently, he is necessarily involved in cramming reluctant people into his idea of the shape of things. When Barnadine understandably declines to provide his own head in lieu of Claudio's, the Duke absurdly complains, 'Unfit to live or die. O gravel heart!' (IV.iii.63). It seems equally bizarre to produce the same Barnadine – a murderer with a most stubbornly anti-social attitude – and set him loose on society in the general orgy of forgiveness at the end of the play: 'But for these earthly faults, I quit them all,/ And pray thee take this mercy to provide/ For better times to come' (V.i.481–3). Here, in the very act of assuming the role of divinity, of delivering and bringing forgiveness for sin, the Duke seems most irresponsible.

Similar complaints have often arisen from the Duke's engineering of the bed-trick. Certainly, the trick is thoroughly legally defensible, converting Angelo's broken betrothal into a binding marriage. The problem is one of fine moral distinctions. Claudio after all is to be beheaded for fornication with a woman whom he had vowed to marry, and who is 'fast [his] wife' (I.ii.136). He is the first victim of the enforcement of the old laws. He suffers on Angelo's direct orders, but indirectly also by the Duke's own will. The Duke now arranges for Angelo to fornicate with Mariana, to whom he was promised in marriage. Whatever the difference in law between a betrothal with and without witnesses, the two fornications seem morally identical: or rather, Claudio's seems preferable since at least he loved Juliet and genuinely wished to marry her. So the Duke seems by the bed-trick to violate his own laws of morality, and to be in some confusion as to whether the result is moral or not. When a messenger enters bearing – as the Duke thinks – Claudio's release as a result of the bed-trick, the Duke says, 'This is his pardon, purchased by such sin/ For which the pardoner himself is in' (IV.ii.106–7). Here at least he seems to perceive that Claudio and

Angelo are morally in the same boat, though he does not recognize that he himself put Angelo there. Earlier, though, persuading Mariana to go along with the idea of sleeping with Angelo, he told her, 'He is your husband on a pre-contract;/ To bring you thus together, 'tis no sin' (IV.i.72–3). Can this mean that it is a sin for Angelo and Mariana, but no sin for the Duke who arranges their meeting?[17]

So long as we try to insist that *Measure for Measure* is a moral and religious allegory of grace superseding justice, with the Duke as a 'power divine', these traditional complaints against the play will continue to be voiced, and it will seem a failure or a very partial success.[18] To silence complaint it is necessary to view the play entirely differently: not as having idealistic goals and failing to meet them, but as pursuing goals which are entirely different.

Viewed as a play of experiment, *Measure for Measure* seems far less problematic. The Duke then becomes, not a human image of divinity at all, but simply an experimenter. However we then respond to his handling of people, we must at least acknowledge that he is entirely true to type, rather than a failure to be what his critics would prefer him to be. Irresponsibility is the very essence of Jacobean moral experiment. It is the nature of the experimenter to want to exploit what he assumes to be the weaknesses of his fellow-men. It is an experimenter's assumption that moral laws are arbitrary that invites an active scientific curiosity about their operation. All this, down to the very uncertain view the experimenter has of his own identity, seems to be true of this play and its hero. On such a view we no longer require Vincentio to be consistent to his own determination to uphold the moral laws, nor complain when he seems to restore all the old laxity at the end. In truth, Vincentio's aims have little to do with the upholding of moral laws. He is interested, not in statesmanship (where he has always been something of a truant), but in specific human cases. The idea of law-enforcement is simply his device to entrap and break Angelo.

His bleak sermon to Claudio on the eve of his execution, delivered at a point in the play prior to his decision to save him, might equally be interpreted as an act of curiosity. After all, Claudio's death seems at this stage to be the price the Duke is prepared to pay for the experiment on Angelo. As yet, Angelo has done no wrong, and so there is as yet no 'reason' to intervene on Claudio's behalf. Until the proof against Angelo arrives, the experiment proceeds unhindered. It is an interesting moral position to be in, to confront the man whose death one is causing, and see if one can persuade him to be 'absolute for death' (III.i.5).

There is, of course, one major difference between this Duke and, say, Webster's Flamineo: Vincentio, having once succeeded in his experiment on Angelo, turns the experiment around, so as to preserve lives, rather than destroy them. He is, after all, a Duke, not a malcontent. Yet the impulse to see what will happen is detectable even as the plot drives towards forgiveness. True, this may not apply to the Duke's pretence that Claudio is dead and Angelo must die for the murder. Only when Isabella's plea for Angelo's life was 'against all reason' would the impulse to forgive be real. In other respects, however, the Duke's engineering of the final events continues to look experimental. What purpose could be served by the initial pretence to side with Angelo against the female plaintiffs, or his encouragement to Angelo to 'punish them to [his] height of pleasure' (V.i.239): unless of course it was to find out just how far Angelo was capable of going? Why, after Isabella has made her plea for Angelo's life should Vincentio pretend to ignore it, and thus to be about to kill Angelo and widow poor Mariana; why pretend to dismiss the provost from his office: unless because of a completely dispassionate curiosity to see how people will behave *in extremis*? Had Vincentio been a different kind of experimenter, he might, as soon as he had known Angelo's proposition to Isabella, have tried to discover if a friar could persuade a nun to go along with the suggestion. As it is, he proposes at the end to see if a novice is prepared to forget her dedication to Christ and take a human husband instead.

In all this, the Duke's own character is virtually non-existent; or rather it switches from scene to scene, according to the exigencies of his own devices. Retiring prince, severe moralist, amoral manipulator, jovial dispenser of bounty, the various roles continually displace each other. The truth is that the man is the experiment. He has no identity beyond his complete absorption in it.

These two very early Jacobean tragicomedies, *The Malcontent* and *Measure for Measure*, provide fascinating proof of how contagious the new impulse was. Shakespeare's is the more interesting case, since he takes an original story (*Promos and Cassandra*) which, for all its crudity, is an honest-to-goodness tale of deliverance and mercy, in which the King operates only according to the information he receives, into a disguised duke plot with the Duke as manipulator and experimenter. Shakespeare has been much praised for the major change to the old story which made Isabella into a nun in her novitiate, and for sparing her chastity by the device of the bed-trick. His theological concern, with the theme of justice and mercy, has frequently been pointed out. Yet, at times, the evident use of Vincentio as experimenter seems greatly at odds with the idealism on which Shakespeare is congratulated. In the case of *The Malcontent*, the evident relish and skill with which the disguised duke enjoys his malcontended and manipulative role seem likewise at odds with the piety on which Marston congratulates himself.

Both dramatists may have been tempted to try out the drama of experiment within the relatively safe form of tragi-comedy, knowing that they could go a good part of the way towards the normally lethal consequences of experimental drama, and then rescue everything with a happy ending. What they were probably unprepared for was how difficult it is to submerge the anarchy of experiment and disguise it as idealism. All the problems which audiences have found with both plays evolve from precisely this source, but it is impossible to regret that they made their experiments. In their different ways, they help prove how impossible it was to put the genie back in the bottle.

3
The Revenger's Tragedy

Self-evidently, *The Revenger's Tragedy* belongs in some sense to the revenge-play genre. This puts it in a tradition which stretches back at least as far as *The Spanish Tragedy*. Yet, one of the oddities of the history of that genre is that, though *The Spanish Tragedy* was universally known and quoted, frequently revived and subsequently refurbished, its immediate progeny was rather meagre. It released no flood of revenge plays, and not until the turn of the century was another major play written in the genre. One possible explanation is that the potential subversiveness of the revenge ethic was better adapted to a later age, more willing to exploit it. Until then, it was likely to remain more or less dormant.

The danger of the revenge play lies in the ambiguous responses evoked towards an avenger. Revenge is forbidden by both human and divine precept. Yet, when human law seems to offer no redress for a wrong, the revenger can plausibly represent himself as the rightful agent of the force of justice. His claim is the more believable since he is subject to a strong call of allegiance from the original victim, who cries out for revenge; a call objectified in the convention of the stage ghost. The avenger seems 'prompted' in his revenge by that near relation to divine will, the power of Fate, as objectified in the strong pull of circumstances in his favour, which seem to offer his quarry into his hands. By the nature of his task, he must embark on a mission which is secretive and inventive; the very essence of the stage avenger's role. So far, his call on an audience's sympathy seems nothing if not sanctioned by righteousness. However, the avenger also releases in an audience a train of response which is far more illicit. In effect, by the essential plot of paying back a wrong, he becomes the vicarious agent to pay back his audience's wrongs. By a kind of transference, he repays all his viewers' own grievances and frustrations, which 'the system' has been unable or reluctant to redress. He obscurely releases a sense of restoring things to rights, and even the most respectable of audiences is accordingly willing to sanction him in the use of whatever means he chooses. Those means are almost invariably violent and remorseless. At the end of the play he must of course be disowned, as objectified by his required death. In the meantime, he may do as he pleases, with the audience's consent. In this usually unacknowledged impulse towards destruction lies the moral danger of the form, and the Jacobean dramatists seize on the revenge format as the perfect instrument to lure their willing viewers into increasingly untenable positions. Using the sympathy generated by the avenger's wrongs, they implicate them in a series of moral experiments.[1]

In *The Revenger's Tragedy*,[2] the motif of moral experimentation is found in a particularly 'pure' form, in the attempted prostitution of Castiza. Vindice gains employment as pimp to Lussurioso, son of the Old Duke, his true enemy. The job gains him access to the court, after nine years' absence, and hence a new chance to get near his enemy. However, his first commission as a 'Piato' is somewhat unexpected:

> LUSSURIOSO
> We thank thee, and will raise thee: receive her name:
> It is the only daughter to Madam Gratiana, the late widow.
> VINDICE (*aside*)
> Oh, my sister, my sister!

> (I.iii.123–5)

Lussurioso then makes the helpful suggestion that Gratiana herself might give a helping hand.

From the start, the idea generates a kind of excitement in Vindice: 'O,/ Now let me burst, I've eaten noble poison;/ . . . Swear me to foul my sister!' While he does speak of his fury at the idea, outrage subsides remarkably quickly, and is replaced by something far more dispassionate:

> And yet, now angry froth is down in me,
> It would not prove the meanest policy
> In this disguise to try the faith of both.
> Another might have had the selfsame office,
> Some slave, that would have wrought effectually,
> Ay, and perhaps o'erwrought 'em; therefore I,
> Being thought travel'd, will apply myself
> Unto the selfsame form, forget my nature,

As if no part about me were kin to 'em;
So tough 'em – though I durst, almost for good,
Venture my lands in heaven upon their blood.

(165–82)

The 'almost' is telling, and the statement of faith is anyway a routine afterthought. Faith in the sacred ties of kinship might be expected here, and Castiza, true to her name, is the most virtuous of sisters. Instead, faith seems almost an irrelevance. Vindice is not even governed by that opposite sensation to faith, by suspicion; but by curiosity. Since he is 'thought travelled' (this was the story he gave out at home), he will indeed put an objective distance between himself and his kin. He will experiment with his sister's virtue, and his mother's integrity. He proceeds to apply himself to his unnatural task with diligence and talent, as if to make sure the experiment is not distorted by brotherly qualms. To his rather hysterical relief, his sister holds out against him. The next stage is to test his mother, using the excuse that the process is merely 'for the salvation of [his] oath' (to Lussurioso). Unfortunately, his mother proves far more pliant. She agrees, for money, to prostitute her own daughter. Vindice's reaction, as it becomes apparent that he is succeeding, is intriguingly mixed:

GRATIANA
    Oh heavens! this overcomes me!
VINDICE (*aside*).
    Not, I hope, already?
GRATIANA
    It is too strong for me; men know that know us,
    We are so weak their words can overthrow us.
    He touch'd me nearly, made my virtues 'bate,
    When his tongue struck upon my poor estate.
VINDICE (*aside*)
    I e'en quake to proceed, my spirit turns edge.
    I fear me she's unmother'd; yet I'll venture.
    "That woman is all male whom none can enter." –
    What think you now lady? Speak, are you the wiser?

(II.i.103–12)

Undoubtedly, Vindice is horrified by the reaction he has produced: but his horror is unequal to suppress his fascinated curiosity. His aphorism about the penetrability of women is a kind of scientific proposition, of which he must now produce the experimental proof. He quakes to proceed: but he does still venture. Later on, he can always convert his mother at sword-point.[3]

The existence here of a motif of moral experiment surely depends on there being little sense of natural feeling. Vindice has not even a shadow of prior suspicion of his mother or his sister to excuse his tamperings. What is lacking is any sense of commitment to them or of involvement with them.[4] There is no allegiance at all, and therefore no inhibition. Vindice is free to 'be' whoever he wants to be; to adopt any role he chooses, and try any identity. It is no accident, then, that the most prominent train of imagery in the play is the imagery of theatre itself. Tourneur goes out of his way to remind us constantly of a sense of the histrionic; either by deliberately exaggerating the theatrical devices he inherits, or by making the characters themselves speak the language of theatre. He inherits the device of the play within the play (from *The Spanish Tragedy* or *Hamlet*), and redoubles it; so that the eventual mass murders of Act Five take place in a masque within a masque within a play.[5] The skull (an obvious borrowing from *Hamlet*) is carried on at the beginning of the play, and becomes an actor in its own drama of revenge. Formerly the skull of the innocent Gloriana, it is dressed up in the clothes of a bashful innocent, and used to poison the Old Duke. When Vindice brings on the disguised skull to try out its effect on his brother Hippolito, he makes it enact a little drama for his benefit:

VINDICE.
  Madame, his grace will not be absent long. –
  Secret? Ne'er doubt us madam. 'Twill be worth
  Three velvet gowns to your ladyship – Known?
  Few ladies respect that disgrace: a poor thin shell!
  'Tis the best grace you have to do it well.
  I'll save your hand that labour, I'll unmask you. [*reveals the skull*]
HIPPOLITO
  Why, brother, brother!
VINDICE
  Art thou beguiled now?

(III.v.43–50)

The Duke, during his own death-scene, not only becomes an actor in a pre-rehearsed drama of revenge – fitting highly predictably into the role chosen for him – but also the enforced spectator of another scene. Vindice and Hippolito force him to watch as the Duchess, and the Duke's own bastard son, Spurio, meet to finalize their plans for incest. Vindice had known beforehand where they would meet, and arranged the Duke's assignation with Castiza to coincide with it. He dies to another stage-reference, by Vindice: 'When the bad bleeds, then is the tragedy good' (III.v.199).

There is another rehearsal scene at the very beginning of Act Five, this time involving the Duke's corpse. The plan is to dress it up in the clothes of 'Piato', and deceive Lussurioso (now Piato's enemy), who will tell Vindice and Hippolito to stab his own father's body. Vindice 'blocks' the scene thus:

> VINDICE
> So, so, he leans well; take heed you wake him not,
> brother.
> HIPPOLITO I warrant you, my life for yours.
> VINDICE
> That's a good lay, for I must kill myself.
> Brother, that's I: that sits for me; do you mark it. And I
> must stand ready here to make away myself yonder. I must
> sit to be killed, and stand to kill myself.

He only regrets that Lussurioso will not be alone and unguarded. Then, he could have attacked him, 'and in catastrophe slain him over his father's breast'. The theatre-vocabulary here seems to indicate that Vindice conceives the idea of killing Lussurioso in terms of 'play'. When he finally accomplishes Lussurioso's murder, it is the same:

> *The Revengers dance. At the end, steal out their swords, and*
> *these four kill the four at the table, in their chairs. It thunders.*
> VINDICE. Mark thunder!
> Dost know thy cue, thou big-voic'd crier? . . .
> When thunder claps, heaven likes the tragedy.

(V.iii.42–8)

Heaven becomes first a stage-hand operating the thunder-run, and then an appreciative audience for Vindice's punning 'play'-murders.

There are two more references before the end of the play to the vocabulary of theatre: to 'piteous tragedy', and to 'tragic bodies'; and Lussurioso's last words are from Seneca.

Not surprisingly, with such an awareness of theatre within the play, its characters inevitably conceive of their lives in terms of role and of spectacular. Even Junior's execution is imagined in terms of a scaffold and a 'gaping people' (III.iii.20). The same impulse is implicit in the play's dedication to revelry. These are all occasions of the greatest ostentation, and imply a constant sense of public performance. Yet it is during these scenes that all the play's major mischiefs occur; as if sin is a public scene. We hear of the rape of Antonio's wife 'When music was heard loudest, courtiers busiest,/ And ladies great with laughter' (I.iv.38–9). Spurio imagines that he was illegitimately conceived 'when deep healths went round,/ And ladies' cheeks were painted red with wine,/ Their tongues as short and nimble as their heels' (I.ii.181–3). The Duke is murdered to the sound of loud music, and his funeral is celebrated, by order of his heir, with revels. During these revels, seven murders are committed, and the assumption is that, 'In this time of revels tricks may be set afoot' (V.i.167). It is the license of carnival extended to homicide: murder as play.

Those revels also give a considerable sense of instability as they are described. Vindice speaks of 'the stirring meats/ Ready to move out of the dishes/ That e'en now quicken when they're eaten!' (II.i.196–8). Spurio goes one step further, and imagines that food could be so 'stirring' that it could directly be the 'first father' of his conception (I.ii.181). The feasting has a kind of active and transforming power. Indeed, revelry can metamorphose whole landscapes: 'I have seen patrimonies wash'd a-pieces,/ Fruit fields turn'd into bastards,/ And in a world of acres, Not so much dust due to th'heir 'twas left to/ As would well gravel a petition' (I.iii.51–4). However, the same fields which have disintegrated into dust, or been converted into bastards, can also be reconstituted, made into goods again: 'I would raise my state upon her breast,/ And call her eyes my tenants; I would count/ My yearly maintenance upon her cheeks,/ Take coach upon her lip and all her parts/ Should keep men after men, and I would ride/ In pleasure upon pleasure' (II.i.94–9). Others 'walk with a hundred acres on their backs' (212). Nothing, however, seems permanent and solid. Rather, the solid seems capable of ruin and re-creation in the same time-scale of instants which mark the moments of sexual pleasure.

Accordingly, human nature itself is easy to transform. Gold 'will quickly enter any man' (I.iii.87),. and 'a right good woman in these days is chang'd/ Into white money with less labour far' (II.ii.26–7). The pace of change and of revelry is frantic: 'Banquets abroad by torch-light, musics, sports . . . / Nine coaches waiting – hurry, hurry, hurry' (II.i.199, 202); 'Now cuckolds are/ A-coining, apace, apace, apace, apace!' (II.ii.142). All energy is focused on 'this present minute' (I.iii.26), the 'vicious minute' (I.iv.39), 'this luxurious day in which we breathe' (I.iii.110). The sense of a stable past as any kind of anchor or restraint is entirely lost.

This factor is crucial in determining the characters' sense of an identity; or rather the lack of it. Our identities are our past. That is what makes us stable, recognizable, consistent people. What we do in the future is conditioned by that past. Yet, in this play, where time seems to accelerate, and to compel all the creatures of the court to live by instants, there is no such sense of a stabilizing past. At times, it seems as if memory itself lapses; and this includes even the memory of absolutely central vows and concepts. Liberated from any sense of a past, the characters can instead play out their charades without restraint.

The most spectacular example of a failing memory comes from Vindice. One would assume that the revenge for Gloriana's death was absolutely central to his existence. He has been carrying her skull around for nine years, plotting his revenge, and it seems crucial to him that he accomplish that revenge himself. He longs for nine years' revenge to crowd into a moment; one of the few references to 'moments' of time which contain also a sense of a past. Yet, in the scene where Lussurioso is arrested for the armed invasion of his step-mother's bedroom, having expected to find Spurio in bed with her but instead finding only his father, Vindice grumbles, 'Would he had killed him; 'twould have eas'd our swords' (II.iii.34). In that moment, the exquisite, crafted revenge is suddenly and casually dismissed. Vindice no longer seems interested; or, at least, it doesn't seem to matter to him how the Old Duke dies.

Similarly, Lussurioso's own memory is fallible. It is he who advises Vindice to use a mother as the best aid to sexual corruption, and seems to scorn Vindice for not having the wit to see its obvious effectiveness. Yet, when Vindice announces that Gratiana proved most obliging in the attempt on Castiza, Lussurioso marvels at the un-heard-of wickedness of such an idea: 'I never thought their sex had been a wonder/ Until this minute' (II.ii.34–5).

Spurio speaks truth in more senses than he knows when he describes himself as 'an uncertain man/ Of more uncertain woman' (I.ii.134–5). Representing himself initially as a committed machiavellian, he nevertheless seems overcome with coyness at the Duchess' incestuous propositions. He speaks of blushing, and contemplates his own potential moral surrender with an ecstasy of excited apprehension: 'O, one incestuous kiss plucks open hell' (I.ii.174). In his soliloquy at the end of the scene, he restores his sense of ruthless evil, with a twist of his own: 'Stepmother, I consent to thy desires;/ I love thy mischief well, but I hate thee,/ And those three cubs thy sons, wishing confusion,/ Death, and disgrace may be their epitaphs'. He certainly acts promptly on what looks like a good opportunity to murder Lussurioso. However, in the scene where the Duke is forced to witness the next assignation with the Duchess, Spurio has to be wooed all over again: 'Had not that kiss a taste of sin, 'twere sweet' (III.v.201). He even thinks of losing his place in heaven, by so wronging his father. The Duchess finally cures his scruples by her persuasive tongue: 'Forget him, or I'll poison him' (208)! It is never clear in all this whether Spurio's moments of modesty are simply meant to stimulate the Duchess; whether his sense of his own evil is a delusion; or whether he can be both evil and bashful. However, the answer is probably that consistency of character is not only insignificant in such a context, but actually unattainable. There is none of the sense of the past and of memory that would sustain it.

What is left is only role and game; each as insubstantial as the various phantom figures who enter the play: Piato, or the four in the masque who slip into the interstices of revelry and leave four unexplained corpses behind them. That sense of insubstantiality is true even of the virtuous. It is not merely that Castiza has a well-developed sense of grievance about money, or that she can on demand play the part of whore so well (in a good cause; the testing of her mother's newly-formed repentance).[6] It is that she conceives even of her own innocence in terms of role, as she reveals in a bitter pun: lamenting that a maiden has 'no other child's-part but her honour' (II.i.3). The wicked have a still better-developed sense of life as a series of arbitrary roles. It has often been remarked that there is an ironic gap between moral pronouncement and immoral action. The theme of the play is not, however, hypocrisy. Rather, it studies morality as impulse. Spurio twice refers to the rape he has committed as 'sport', and protests that he dies for doing what every woman wants. The Duchess, reacting to the Old Duke's failure to reprieve Spurio from the rape charge, vows 'And therefore wedlock faith shall be forgot' (I.ii.106). She apparently plans her first adultery as a retaliation. Yet, as she sees Spurio now approaching, she says, 'And here comes he whom my heart points unto,/ His bastard son, but my love's true-begot;/ Many a wealthy letter have I sent him,/ Swell'd up with jewels, and the timorous man/ Is yet but coldly kind./ That jewel's mine that quivers in his ear' (109–14). So, the motive of revenge is casually draped over an *existing* lust. Various other 'revenge' impulses seem equally irrational. After the death of Junior, killed in effect by his brothers who thought they had instead achieved the execution in prison of Lussurioso, one of the brothers comes out with what has been described as a startling moral perception: 'there is nothing sure in mortality/ But mortality' (III.vi.86–7). However, he immediately follows it with, 'Well, no more words; shalt be revenged i'faith'. It is hard to see how the proposed second strike against Lussurioso can be described as a revenge against their own stupidity. The 'therefore's' of revenge, at their best, follow their own logic. Here they seem especially insane. Once again, the most absorbing instance is found to be in Vindice, in the episode concerning Castiza. He has been commissioned to corrupt her: 'therefore I,/ Being thought travell'd, will . . . forget my nature' (I.iii.177–9). He has received an invitation to play, to experiment. The power of impulse in this play ensures that it is not a temptation he will decline. That is the only necessary logic in his 'therefore'.

As to his own identity in that process, it becomes intriguingly clear that there is no certainty whether that identity can be regarded as internal or external. As he tries to pervert his mother into a procuress, and therefore has to cope with a quite new view of her, he has an interesting technique for protecting himself; a kind of retreat. He begs heaven to 'turn the precious side/ Of both my eyeballs inward, not to see myself' (II.i.127–8). Yet the idea is a curious reversal of the normal idea that the true self lies within. Vindice seems to accept that his 'self' is his outside; in which case, he 'is' his disguise. Trying to decide whether or not to embark on the whole experiment, it is finally to his disguise, rather than to any other 'self', that he decides to be 'true' (II.ii.38).

A rather similar case is found with Gratiana. Falling to the trade of procuress for presumably the first time, she adopts it with talent; as if the persona were ready-formed in her mind, and available to play. This would seem to imply an 'identity' which is a matter of role-selection. Castiza pretends not to see her mother in front of her, and then demands, 'Mother, come from that poisonous woman there . . . Do you not see her? She's too inward then' (II.i.234–5). The mother is within, but the corrupt outer shape threatens to invade her. However, later, Vindice seems to speak of an opposite process: 'For in that shell of mother breeds a bawd' (IV.iv.10). It is not clear whether the mother is the inner or the outer 'self'.

The ultimate case of a character confusing role with self is Vindice's final speech, when he speaks of his folly at disclosing his own crimes, but suddenly thinks of 'Piato':

> Now I remember too, here was Piato
> Brought forth a knavish sentence once;
> No doubt (said he) but time
> Will make the murderer bring forth himself.
> 'Tis well he died; he was a witch.

(V.iii.113–17)

'Piato' was the name of the disguise he himself adopted for Lussurioso's benefit at first, yet here he seems to believe in Piato as a real figure with a real death; a figure quite separate from 'himself' (whoever that self might be).

Given that the self is invariably considered in terms of role, and that play and experiment correspondingly become the dominant motivations of all characters, it is hardly surprising that the predominant tone of the play is somewhere between horror and hilarity.[7] It is impossible, given such a world, for any single character actively involved in it to take seriously the values of a moral scheme or of a human life. As Vindice witnesses the death of the Old Duke, his only true enemy in the play, he is already making up a new game, with new rules: 'The dukedom wants a head, thou' yet unknown:/ As fast as they peep up, let's cut 'em down' (III.v.219–20). Clearly, he thinks that this proposed harvest of heads is a good joke, and jokes are usually most prevalent in the play in the scenes of greatest violence. There are several rather good ones during the murder-scene of the Old Duke, from the reference to Castiza's dressed-up skull as 'the bony lady', and the announcement of 'her' to the Duke as having 'somewhat a *grave* look with her', to the wisecrack about the Duke's teeth being eaten away by the poison: "'twill teach you to kiss closer,/ Not like a slobbering Dutchman'. As Nicholas Brooke has so aptly remarked, 'laughter and horror . . . hardley seem to be opposed: they are so closely allied that laughter becomes the only possible expression of the horror, not in any possible sense, a relief'. Horror, however, is not the reaction of the characters themselves, nor of the author, nor rarely in any simple sense of the audience or reader. 'Horror' becomes a merely theoretical normal response, distantly alluded to in the moral clichés spouted by the immoral. The same people who utter the clichés are most 'ravished' by the next invitation to immoral game.

They have this much justification: that in a world which has already become grotesque, and in which somehow they must survive, the only possible response to extravagant evil and suffering is the laughter of the absurd. Not even one's own life can be taken seriously, let alone a set of moral imperatives. Energies become entirely dedicated to a demonstration of the complete absurdity of that world, and derision is the natural language of that endeavour.

This is even true of the references the play makes to a divinity. On the face of it, Vindice comes increasingly to realize not only that the court is corrupt, even by the standards of *this* world, but that there is another possible world to oppose to it. His 'sermons' over the skull in III.v seem to concentrate as never before on the skull as an emblem of mortality which reproaches even himself. Like a preacher of a former age, he concentrates all the force of his perception of the mortality of man to demonstrate the vanity of all human preoccupations. The skull confronts the flesh, in all the flesh's sensuality and gluttony, and reminds it to what it will one day come. Is it for *this* that flesh feeds itself? Vindice entertains himself with the thought of the skull appearing at banquets and brothels, to freeze the sinner with fear even in the act of sin.[8] Yet the point of his tirade is finally no more than another form of self-gratification. He enjoys the superiority of every humorist, and his pleasure in the speech is at least half masturbatory.[9] At best, it is a rapturous feat of rhetorical skill. No more than anyone else in the play does Vindice here allow his pleasures of the present moment to be disturbed by a genuine sense of the longer perspectives of time.

The play seems entirely to justify him in this respect. There are three direct manifestations of 'God' in the play: two claps of thunder and a blazing star. All three come during ominous moments, just before the cleansing of the court by murder. If we can at all expect heaven to condone such a process, we might anticipate that this would be the preface – on the parallel of an earlier drama – to the enactment on stage of the Christian patterns of sin/hell, virtue/ heaven. The painted 'heavens' above the stage, and the diabolic cellarage below it, traditionally invoked those patterns, and the plays frequently enacted them. Marlowe's Dr Faustus has forfeited his soul to Satan, and is duly carried off at the end of the play by a devil, into a stage representation of hell-mouth. The figure of 'Revenge', in The Spanish Tragedy, vows to the ghost of the wronged Andrea, 'To place thy friends in ease, the rest in woes:/ For here though death hath end their misery,/ I'll there begin their endless tragedy'. It is an interesting echo here, of the traditional christian definition of comedy and tragedy. In Jacobean drama, however, those terms become exclusively theatrical in reference; and the christian eschatology also becomes part of a merely theatrical pattern. There is no sense of an afterlife alluded to, beyond the play. Heaven and hell are *within* the play. When the Old Duke is suffering his death agonies, he cries, 'Is there a hell besides this, villains?' (III.v.182). The answer seems to be, 'no'.

Irony always creates an enclosed pattern, of mocking response to confident wish. Impulse recoils on itself: it is this which makes the pattern enclosed. The irony by which the Old Duke dies (murder in lust, for murder in lust; poison, for poison) is entirely self-enclosed in this way. The whole play is full of such ironic reversals, often hilarious.[10] The best example is probably when the brothers discover that, after all their hypocritical concern, the jailor actually has Junior's severed head, not Lussurioso's, in his bag, and yell, 'Villain, I'll brain thee with it' (III.vi.78). What this means is that there is no need, as was the case in earlier plays, to invoke heaven's aid in producing a satisfying catastrophe for the wicked. The in-built mechanisms of the absurd world of the play ensure this without any god. So, when a god does seem to appear in the play, it turns out that he is at the beck and call of sardonic mortals. Notably, when Vindice calls on heaven for a thunder-clap, it obliges. It seems to be at his personal command. What is more, it responds to a summoner who treats it sardonically: 'Is there no thunder left, or is't kept up/ In stock for heavier vengeance? (*Thunder.*) There it goes!' (IV.ii.193–4). It even comes directly on theatrical cue – 'Dost know thy cue, thou big-voic'd crier?' (V.iii.43) – which establishes heavenly justice as one more agent in a theatrical black farce. When justice finally comes to Vindice himself, it is as the last self-enclosed irony of that farce, when he foolishly confesses to Antonio his role as multiple murderer; forgetting that Antonio, as new Duke, now has a position to keep up in the world. Only then does the gleeful playing of roles, games and experiments have to end, and Vindice fittingly greets his own death as being as arbitrary and as hilarious as any other.

That sense of indifference fits the sense the play seems to convey of life as role. It is only the virtuous who are confined to a single 'part', like Castiza and her 'child's part', her honour. Others are free to enjoy multiple lives, and are less likely to take any of them with grim seriousness. With its stress on the momentary, and its sense of lightning pace, this play encourages the life of mere impulse, gratification and game. Every moment is therefore experimental, and with the hero protected by his all-licensing revenger's cause, he feels particularly free to manipulate almost every other life into anarchic game; this is particularly true of his experiment with the honour of his own mother and sister, but in effect the wild possibilities he explores with the Old Duke or his son equally prove that Vindice now lives a life of active conjecture. Like his successors, he finds that anything is possible.

4
The White Devil

Much work has been done on establishing the sources of Webster's play, and comparing the sources with the finished product.[1] It appears that Webster's version of the events that had actually taken place in Italy a generation earlier is substantially modified, and that the modifications do more than simply tidy the story up. All subsequent events in Webster's version stem from this murder of Isabella, Duke Brachiano's innocent wife, as the Duke pursues another man's wife, Vittoria, the White Devil of the title. Specifically, there follow the eventual deaths of Brachiano and Vittoria themselves, at the hands of Isabella's brother, Francisco de Medici; deaths which were accounted for quite differently in the main source, where the death of Brachiano especially stemmed from mere natural causes. What this amounts to is that Webster superimposed on a relatively formless, lurid sequence of events, the specific dramatic form of the revenge play. To do so, he invented a main revenger, a new character for Isabella, accomplices for the revenger, an occasion, and a set of revenge-devices.

These devices include the entire apparatus of the conventional revenge play. There are ghosts. Ghosts had been an indispensable part of any revenge play since at least *The Spanish Tragedy*, and of course there is no more famous ghost in all literature than the ghost of Old Hamlet. Webster, making sure that we know what kind of play we're watching, has not one ghost but two. Firstly there is the ghost of Isabella, who appears to her brother Francisco (IV.i). This is a highly traditional appearance of an original murder victim to the victim's chosen instrument of revenge. Secondly, there is the ghost of Brachiano, who appears, to threaten Flamineo (V). Then there is the matter of skulls. No soi-disant revenge play could afford to be without one, especially after *The Revenger's Tragedy*; and *The White Devil* duly follows suit. He not only includes a skull, but combines it with a ghost, Brachiano's (V.iv): '*Enter Brachiano's Ghost, in his leather cassock and breeches, boots, a cowl, a pot of lily-flowers with a skull in't . . . The Ghost throws earth upon him and shows him the skull*'. Webster misses out on the customary play-within-a-play (though there is a dumb-show), but does use the 'mad mother motif'. Actually, his character of Cornelia is a kind of fusion of the mad mother of *The Spanish Tragedy* with the mad daughter Ophelia in *Hamlet*, since there is a good deal of the language of Ophelia in Cornelia's speeches, with bits of Lady Macbeth for good measure. The echoes are particularly unmistakable in her speech, 'Here's Rosemary for you, and Rue for you' just before the entry of Brachiano's ghost; but the whole business of her madness is clearly 'stock', as the stage-direction *'Cornelia doth this in several forms of distraction'* makes clear. The apparatus of revenge is therefore very insistently used. No audience could fail to recognize the kind of play that was being imitated and evoked.

However, it has for long been recognized that Webster substantially modifies his chosen conventions of revenge.[2] The recognition could easily be pressed to the conclusion that, just as Webster includes certain religious rituals in this play only to invert them (marriage, confessional, extreme unction),[3] so, with revenge-play conventions, they are imported only in order to confound the expectations normally aroused by the form. This is entirely fitting for the purposes of a dramatist writing an experimental play.[4] One of the most legitimate devices of a dramatist intent on tampering with established moral responses is to subvert the standard responses of his own medium.[5] Inevitably this will sufficiently unsettle an audience as to make it at least suspend normal judgement. Of course, revenge is itself a highly serviceable medium for moral experiment, as *The Revenger's Tragedy* proves. However, Webster is intent on denying his audience even the spurious righteousness of the revenger. What he has in mind is to make his audience respond to and identify with the original criminals.

What makes this intention clear is the exact correspondence between the central family units in *The Revenger's Tragedy* and *The White Devil*, and the sympathies they generate.[6] In both plays the group involves a mother, two sons and a daughter. In both, the plot involves an attempt by the more malcontented brother to prostitute his sister to a nobleman. In both plays, the balance of good and evil in the family is roughly equal and remains so. The main difference of course is that the sister in Webster's play willingly succumbs. She succumbs to a temptation which is, in this play, in no sense an 'act'. Her brother is wholly committed to her prostitution as an important career gambit, and so there is not the smallest token gesture this time by the central malcontent that he is engaged in any kind of crusade against vice. It follows that good has an even harder task of survival in this play than in Tourneur's, and comprehensively fails. This includes the murder of the 'good' brother by the 'evil' one. Yet, the latter, Flamineo, seems to generate and retain at least as much dramatic sympathy as had his counterpart, Vindice, in *The Revenger's Tragedy*.[7] More significantly still, though she is far less chaste than Castiza in the earlier play, Webster's counterpart to Castiza, Vittoria, is also far more dramatically prominent, to the extent that generations of commentators have been hard pressed to find respectable reasons for responding to her, or have over-emphasized the undoubted negative sides of her presentation.[8] Thus, while a normal revenge play includes an evil-doer, a victim, and a revenger, and invites us to identify with the second and third of these, this play invites our response only to the first. There is little interest or sympathy generated for the victims, and there is a similar neglect of their avengers. Revenge is imported to the story only to be shunted to one side and neglected. The family groupings seem to argue Webster's intention to compel our interest in the same basic set of people as in Tourneur, even when they have no right on their side at all. The revenger has a cause. Flamineo and Vittoria have none. Yet it is Flamineo and Vittoria who claim our attention and even perhaps our respect, rather than their righteous enemies. Every statement made about so subtle a play as *The White Devil* needs to be qualified, but it seems clear that Webster is experimenting with the possibility of pushing dramatic sympathy into a wholly new area. There had of course been many attractive villains in English drama before, but never before had attractive villains taken over a revenge play from an avenger. By extension, what he is also clearly trying to achieve is to make his audience extend their *ethical* tolerance into unheard-of areas. His wish, therefore, expressed in the Preface to the first published edition of the play, to be read by the light of all his more 'respectable' fellow-dramatists, is entirely misleading, and evidently when the play was performed this was fully understood by his audience. The same Preface dolefully complains of the play's failure when it was first performed at the Red Bull Theatre, a recently-built but old-fashioned popular playhouse. Webster offers the explanations that it was winter, and in an open-air theatre at that. However, the explanation that carries most weight is that the popular audience was unsuitable for a play so clearly at odds with conventional forms. They disliked the discomfort of having what was familiar to them disturbed. As is well known, you can persuade intelligent men of anything. Stupid men are harder to convince.

Webster does not, however, try to win our sympathy or interest for Vittoria or Flamineo by simply playing down their guilt. Rather, their guilt is something he absolutely insists on. He makes us aware that both are not only sinners but also criminals. The first of these needs little demonstration. Like *The Revenger's Tragedy*, Webster's play invokes much of the language of the morality drama, particularly in the endless repetitions of the word 'devil', and the preoccupation with death, damnation, and temptation. From the title on, we are kept constantly within a context of these themes. Brachiano's first words are of a man 'quite lost' (I.ii.3), and the impact of his own damnation recurs with renewed force just before his reconciliation with Vittoria in IV.ii: 'How long have I beheld the devil in crystal?/ Thou hast led me like an heathen sacrifice,/ With music and with fatal yokes of flowers,/ To my eternal ruin' (84–7). He is not alone in identifying Vittoria as devil. Monticelso, predictably, uses the same charge more than once in the trial scene, with his righteous insult that, 'Were there a second paradise to lose/ This devil would betray it' (III.ii.69–70). Her own brother had already admiringly described her as an 'excellent devil' (I.ii.249) when her 'dream' had proposed the murder of inconvenient spouses. If indeed she has lured Brachiano to his damnation, the play seems intent on recording the process to its end. Brachiano is seen to his death by his enemies, who insist throughout the process that they are also sending him to hell. Actually, the sins they profess to be sending him to judgement for do not include adultery. To his enemies, Brachiano seems a 'devil' in his own right, with all his arts of poison; and Flamineo in his turn is consigned to hell as just another 'devil' in his first, mock, death in V.vi. Among the play's most famous lines are those death speeches by Vittoria and Flamineo in which they fearfully confess that they do not know what the destination of their souls might be. The obsession with the terms of the christian eschatology is constantly reinforced by the apparatus of the church, whether in the presence of cardinals or a pope, the parody of the last rites, an excommunication, or a House of Convertites. The play practically beats these themes to death.

As to the sense of technically criminal guilt, this too is kept constantly before us, by repeated references, and by an insistent context of law and justice. It has often been commented that Webster recreates with skill a sense of specific historical environment, even at the expense of crowding his plays with gratuitous detail such as the investiture of the Pope, done with antiquarian care.[9] He makes sure that that historical environment comes complete with its apparatus of the law and this ensures that guilt and innocence are given a specifically legal connotation to reinforce the moral judgements passed.

The most obvious example of the process is in the trial of Vittoria, which is given a formal heading in the text ('THE ARRAIGNEMENT OF VITTORIA'), which extends over about 250 lines, and for which the entire cast is assembled. The reverberations of this formal trial are still felt many scenes later, in Vittoria's recall of her trial, and in her attempt to escape the sentence. One of Brachiano's hallucinations, while he is dying from poison, takes the specific form of the law, bribes, lawyer and hanging: 'See, see, Flamineo that kill'd his brother/ Is dancing on the ropes there; and he carries a money-bag in each hand, to keep him even,/ For fear of breaking's neck. And there's a lawyer/ In a gown whipt with velvet, stares and gapes/ When the money will fall. How the rogue cuts capers!/ It should have been in a halter' (V.iii.108–14). If this trial seems to haunt the minds of those involved, it is far from being the only one in the play. The immediate sequel to Vittoria's escape from prison is another sentence. This time, it is pronounced by the Pope, at his investiture which is itself hedged about with laws and precedents. It is a sentence of excommunication for Vittoria and Brachiano, and of banishment for her kin (IV.iii). Earlier, Flamineo had been arrested with his brother on suspicion for the murders of Isabella and Vittoria's husband Camillo (II.ii), and is subsequently banished from the presence by Brachiano's successor, young Giovanni. This banishment is something Flamineo represents in specifically legal terms, punning on the two meanings of the word, 'court', and protesting about a 'court ejectment' being made against him (V.iv.45). The legal term refers to a writ of eviction from land. Complaining that measures should not always be pressed to extreme conclusions, his imagination conjures up another law-related example: 'Say that a gentlewoman were taken out of her bed about midnight and committed to Castle Angelo, to the tower yonder, with nothing about her but her smock; would it not show a cruel part in the gentleman porter to lay claim to her upper garment, pull it o'er her head and ears, and put her in nak'd?' (37–43). The Doctor who is used to procure poison for Isabella (II.i) has just escaped from one charge (lechery) by pretending previous conviction on another (debt). Even when there is no specific legal process in operation, characters' minds often work with the vocabulary of the law, its officers and its sentences. Flamineo, seeking from Vittoria the financial reward he never collected during Brachiano's lifetime, speaks of 'executrix' and 'patent' and the 'public scaffold' and a 'bill of sale' (V.vi). Brachiano's murderers tell him that his lord and master (the devil) is going to the gallows (V.iii), and in their turn are called hangmen when they go to murder Vittoria and Flamineo. Hanging, hangmen and gallows are mentioned nine times through the play; the law and lawyers the same number. When Francisco plots the murder of the newly-married couple, he consults a 'black book' of criminals in the possession of his cardinal-brother, the future Pope, Monticelso. It is a list of those who have escaped justice only to be exploited for future criminal uses by those who hold the power of blackmail over them. Francisco speculates about who the blackmailer might be: 'some cunning fellow/ That's my lord's officer, one that lately skipp'd/ From a clerk's desk up to a justice' chair,/ Hath made this knavish summons' (IV.i.75–8).

The language of the law is actually applied against most of the more powerful or active figures in the play, whether belonging to Vittoria's family or to the families of her enemies. Its effect is to redouble the sense of real wrongdoing, of activities that are at best on the shady side of the law, and frequently in direct conflict with it. None seems better acquainted with the language of the law and its penalties than Flamineo. There can be no dispute about the real guilt of him and his family, however guilty others might also be. R. W. Dent is right to point out that a good deal of Vittoria's guilt remains at the level of hearsay, for us as audience as well as for her accusers.[10] Nevertheless, the link between on the one hand her 'dream' which suggests to Brachiano the idea of murdering her husband and his wife, and on the other their subsequent murders, is strong enough to establish strong circumstantial proof of her complicity. She might have been charged with conspiracy to murder. Instead, she is only tried for immorality. With Flamineo, we actually see him murder his own brother.

Yet these characters command our interest, our involvement, even our respect. They crowd out all the normal responses of the revenge pattern. We should be interested only in their downfall, in revenge being committed against them. Instead, when the revengers come in at the end to kill Flamineo and Vittoria, chanting 'Isabella, Isabella', it may need a considerable feat of memory to recall who Isabella was, and what she has to do with this situation. Her murder had in fact been a particularly heartless one, and Vittoria had been behind it. Yet such is the power of Webster's ethical experiment, that normal moral reactions are confused or even inverted.[11]

Basically, however loudly the voices of religion and the law seem to speak to us in the play, and urge us to condemn the wicked, there is in practice nothing to impel us to heed them. On the contrary, there is everything to urge us to ignore them, when other claims are made on us. If the play constructs a context of religion and law, it nevertheless also constructs a wider context of human relations which deny meaning to the traditional pieties. Solipsism is the constant rule of life for all but the 'good'; and the good are the first to be destroyed. Flamineo states this condition of life most clearly:

> I do not look
> Who went before, nor who shall follow me;
> No, at myself I will begin and end:
> While we look up to heaven we confound
> Knowledge with knowledge.

(V.vi.256–60)

Since these death-speeches of Flamineo are the last lines of any power spoken in the play, they have a compelling extra claim to represent in every sense the play's last word on the topics of the self and the soul. He specifically rejects the claims of religion to represent life's final truths. Such messages are too remote, too confusing. The 'knowledge' which the world provides cannot be ignored, and it conflicts with the simple and reassuring truths of the Bible. He falls back instead on his one certainty: his own self. That is his only certain knowledge.

What is notable is that it is a knowledge which he constantly seeks to extend. Perhaps even more clearly than Vindice, Flamineo represents the impulse of the Jacobean 'hero' to dabble and experiment with morality and with his own moral feelings. One of his most suggestive speeches in the play comes just after he has witnessed his mother's madness, in her grief for his murder of Marcello:

> I have liv'd
> Riotously ill, like some that live in court:
> And sometimes, when my face was full of smiles
> Have felt the maze of conscience in my breast.

Oft gay and honor'd robes those tortures try:
We think cag'd birds sing, when indeed they cry.

(V.iv.116–21)

Noticeably, Flamineo's tender concern is not for the brother he has just killed but for himself. Nevertheless, this is for him an unusual note of even *self*-pity. The image of the caged birds particularly seems to solicit sympathy for his own lot as an isolated captive in an alien court – a court to which he evidently doesn't feel he really belongs, since he compares himself to 'some that live in court'. Yet the previous line contains an interesting ambiguity on the subject of pain. On the face of it, all the line means is that those who wear the trappings of apparent wealth and gaiety may experience the torment of conscience. Yet the word, 'try' seems to imply an element of deliberate 'trial' in the sense of experimentation. Possibly, then, when he says he has felt conscience when his face was full of smiles, he means that he quite consciously provoked situations where he could try out the contrast between face and feeling. The idea of a 'maze' of conscience seems initially to imply only amazement or astonishment at sudden visitations of guilt, however deliberately they had been risked. Yet the 'maze' also seems to refer to the complexity of moral issues; and, in the face of that complexity, as in the face of theological problems, he prefers simply to risk all, and to defy the consequences of what he knows must be evil. Evidently, the process does not protect him from some kind of pain, but he can still function at the level of anarchic experimenter with his own feelings and the fate of others. The proof of this is almost immediately at hand. As if to reinforce his own sense of living riotously ill, Brachiano's ghost enters, and portentously throws earth at him and shows him a skull. It is a visible premonition of Flamineo's own imminent death, decomposition and decay. Yet, Flamineo treats the omen with remarkably little misgiving. In fact, he treats it as a kind of challenge, of the sort presumably which shapes his whole response to life. He knows the risks he runs. His actions constantly give him pain. Yet his response to the risk is to treat it as a kind of test of his defiance: 'Ha! I can stand thee: nearer, nearer yet'. There follows a whole series of wild, mocking questions: 'In what place art thou? in yon starry gallery?/ Or in the cursed dungeon? No? not speak?/ Pray, sir, resolve me, what religion's best/ For a man to die in?' In view of the play's saturation with the terms of Christian eschatology, it is particularly interesting to find that heaven and hell are named only in terms of the geography of the theatre, as had been the case with *The Revenger's Tragedy*. So soon after his confession of the pangs of conscience, and at the very point where he might be expected to feel most aware of the welfare of his soul, conventional concern dissolves into whimsy and provocation. He pushes his luck with the ghost until he gets earth thrown at him and the skull revealed. The questions about low long he has to live, the 'Most necessary question', seems not to be all-important. The earth thrown at him he knows to be 'fatal', but he jumps off to ask about dead men and their 'familiars'. In other words, mere self-preservation is immediately displaced by a kind of hilarious curiosity, which actually succeeds in driving off the ghost. Its disappearance simply confirms Flamineo in his defiance: 'I do dare my fate/ To do its worst'. Defiance and experimentation are surely connected. Flamineo's only real motive is to see how far he can go, how much he can get away with. It is an enterprise of such moral wildness that his invariable idiom lies in the absurd.[12]

Nowhere is this impulse more evident than in the murder of his brother, which differs from the murder of other brothers in Elizabethan or Jacobean drama by its complete and intentional motivelessness. No doubt Flamineo finds Marcello's rectitude to be an irritating priggishness; but he seems more than capable of handling that. The quarrel over Zanche (V.i), however, seems to give him an opportunity to play out an arbitrary and violent farce with his brother. It is not, as has been claimed before, that he needs simply to destroy a good life which reproaches his, or that he is angry because a humour of his has been thwarted. Rather, the impulse he feels is to discover if he can without feeling and without real motive suppress or destroy one of the closest ties that bind him. His wish is to see if he can exist alone, untrammelled by feelings or relationships. The truest solipsist in the whole corpus of Elizabethan or Jacobean drama, there is from him, when the process is complete, no pathetic lament that 'there is no creature loves me'. Rather, his whole endeavour seems to be increasingly to isolate himself from others. After his brother's murder, his next aim is deliberately to alienate himself from his sister, his only hope of protection now that Brachiano, too, is dead. The experiment in the violation of moral feeling is however at its purest with the good Marcello.

Accordingly, the quarrel about Zanche comes immediately after he has himself assured Zanche in the plainest terms that his appetite for her is dead. When Marcello kicks the insolent Zanche, and then tries to reproach his brother for the family disgrace of sleeping with a black, it is Flamineo who pushes the quarrel to the point of no return. His escalating accusations of childishness, effeminacy, and finally bastardy succeed in provoking Marcello into issuing a challenge. It is all the warrant Flamineo needs. He had no previous notion of killing his brother. There is now no recorded process of moral decision. Dramatic time is deliberately and fully contracted so that while, at the beginning of the next scene, Cornelia speaks of hearing court rumours about the quarrel, we have no sense of any intervening pause before Flamineo now enters, walks briskly up to his brother, comments, 'I have brought your weapon back', and '*runs* Marcello *through*'. This 'murder in jest' is evidently done so completely without feeling that, when his mother dares to cry murder, his response to her is, 'Do you turn your gall up?' The phrase has been interpreted as referring to Marcello 'turning up his toes', but seems rather to refer to Cornelia, and to snarl or sneer at her horror as some kind of unwarranted nagging. Flamineo exits, but within a few minutes is back again with Brachiano, making the offhand comment that the murder was a bit of bad luck ('It was my misfortune'), and observing completely neutrally and silently his mother's anguished grief. He seems surprised when Brachiano grants only a conditional pardon for the murder.

The long death-scenes of Brachiano now intervene, but finally, in V.iv, Flamineo is told that his mother has gone mad with grief. He insists on seeing her, even though he is told that the sight of him will increase her distress. For once, he gets more sensation than he can deal with. Half-way through the scene, he says 'I would I were from hence', but has to endure the sight of his mother's madness for another twenty lines. When finally she has left, he confesses that he feels some strange feeling: 'I have a strange feeling in me, to th'which/ I cannot give a name, without it be/ Compassion'. The clever isolation of the last word at the beginning of another line signals to the actor the intended pause, as Flamineo gropes for the right word. It might almost emerge as a question, since obviously he has never felt anything like it before, and has no name for it. He has tried to see if he actually had any of the feelings of which others spoke. Only now, with a brother murdered and a mother driven mad, does he finally discover in himself an unsullied emotion.

In the light of this scene it may be possible to arrive at a closer definition of exactly what his 'moral experiment' consists of. It seems not to be, finally, externally directed. There is no real wish to show the world the absurdity of its own moral vocabulary, and least of all is there the urge to do violence for any political end. On the contrary, all Flamineo's cynical comments on others' failings continue to draw on the traditional vocabulary. His tirades on hypocrisy, particularly, are based on the commonplace assumption that true feelings are available to men and are preferable to false shows. His ambitions for court reward are not only conventional but essentially tend to be conservative of the political order in which his efforts are invested. However, ambition is not a wholly adequate fulfilment of his energies, and the experiment which finally takes precedence over it will always in the end conflict with it.

That experiment is internally directed, and the knowledge it seeks is of the extremes of the self. Flamineo has always known the concepts of right and wrong, and has experienced moral confusion, the 'maze of conscience'. His reaction has been to defy that conscience; to 'try' it; to violate it; and to record the response. It is a form of driving deep into his own mind's privacy, and these responses are the true subject-matter of the experiment. Ultimately, he wants to find out if his mind possesses such a thing as feeling for others. He forces himself to commit the kind of atrocities which will prove the discovery either way. Paradoxically, the discovery almost by definition involves the *destruction* of others, but perhaps for Flamineo this is incidental. Only his own mind matters. The violation of others, the consequent increased isolation of the self, tend if anything to concentrate that self-obsession.

After the disappearance of Brachiano's ghost, Flamineo decides to approach Vittoria, explain his ejection from the court and the dire spiritual condition he is in, and demand financial help. Undoubtedly, Flamineo is in real financial distress. His hopes of reward died with Brachiano; and while Zanche is able to offer abundant wealth to her new lover Lodovico, Flamineo has evidently done much less well out of the court. However, if reward is his true motive, he employs strange means to achieve it. Right from the beginning of his interview with Vittoria and Zanche, he behaves so belligerently that Vittoria asks if he is drunk, and calls him 'ruffian'. He shoves a pen and paper before her and demands that, as executrix of Brachiano's will, she write down what she will give him. Not surprisingly, she responds by bequeathing him the legacy of Cain. But then, his real motive seems to be to provoke one final quarrel, and to break his final human tie. He comes equipped with pistols. He expects to use them, and not merely to get money with menaces. He very rapidly achieves that, with Vittoria abruptly changing her tune: 'What would you have me do?/ Is not all mine, yours?' (V.vi.29–30). He could have stopped there, and got his money, but what he proceeds with is a carefully planned experiment. Abruptly switching direction, he tells her that he is about to fulfil Brachiano's dying wish, that neither Vittoria nor he, Flamineo, should survive him. Flamineo already anticipates that the two women will try instead to murder him. The experiment is to prove it, and when he has done so he hints – 'I live/ To punish your ingratitude' – that he will now murder them. His plan gives him an ironic perspective on all their efforts to save their skins, since they behave exactly as he predicts. The pistols are loaded only with blanks, enabling him to seem to trust their sudden promise that it is their greatest wish to die, so long as he dies first and shows them how to do it. When they shoot him, stamp on his body, and gleefully consign him to hell, he can give a hilarious pastiche of bewildered and painful death throes, more or less inviting them to convict themselves more and more fully. Then, he gets up, and tells them there were no bullets.

He uses the very language of experiment: 'now I have tried your love. . . . 'Twas a plot to prove your kindness to me'. He begins with the proposition that women are untrustworthy, and sets out to provide the experimental proof. His response is not remotely one of horror. In fact, he seems delighted by what he has observed: 'How cunning you were to discharge! Do you practise at the Artillery Yard?' He also believes he has discovered more than that a woman has ways of defending herself. After all, they did more than simply shoot him. They murdered him in a spirit of such venomous laughter as to prove themselves his own true spiritual kin. Vittoria murders, and feels enhanced by doing so: 'This thy death/ Shall make me like a blazing ominous star:/ Look up and tremble'. Another 'proof' that Flamineo extracts from the experiment is that husbands would do well to ignore their wives' protestations of undying love. After all, Vittoria had pretended to die *for Brachiano*. She had made a display of devotion: 'Behold, Brachiano, I that while you liv'd/ Did make a flaming altar of my heart/ To sacrifice unto you; now am ready/ To sacrifice heart and all'. Flamineo concludes that the love was as false as the show: 'Trust a woman? never, never. Brachiano be my precedent: we lay our souls to pawn to the devil for a little pleasure, and a woman makes the bill of sale'. These discoveries provide Flamineo with a kind of final confirmation that the condition of life he faces is utterly solitary, and all relationships illusory. His logical response to this proof is that this stranger/sister must die, and he is indignant that the entry of Lodovico and his cronies means he will not be able to kill Vittoria himself.

She has proved herself, however, essentially like him. There are three occasions in the play where we might detect moments of moral hesitation in Vittoria. All are unexpected. The first comes when her mother overhears, in I.ii, the interview with Brachiano, including the 'dream'. Flamineo behaves here as he does later towards his mother. He consciously and sneeringly violates all her dearly-held moral standards. Vittoria, however, falters, apologises, pleads extenuation, and then runs from the stage with words that leave an impression of at least regret at hurting her mother: 'O me accurs'd' (294). She repeats the same exclamation on the death of Brachiano, in what seems to be an outburst of genuine grief: 'O me! this place is hell' (V.iii.176). On her own death, she comes out with a self-accusation, though a mitigating one: 'O, my greatest sin lay in my blood./ Now my blood pays for it' (V.vi.240–1). These three occasions of scruple or feeling perhaps establish her as a far less self-knowing character than Flamineo.[13] Clearly she is guilty of more than sins of the 'blood', but seems unaware of her own deviousness. Her outburst of grief for Brachiano seems at odds with everything else we see of her manipulative relationship with him. Her scruples about offending her mother do nothing to change her course of life. Evidently, 'feeling' is something that comes to her readily, and means perhaps little within the general context of her role-playing. However, the three occasions also correspond, in however lightweight a way, to her brother's momentary confessions of moral scruple or quest for feeling. The response is also the same. In no sense can Vittoria be regarded as an innocent. Given the perfect opportunity to kill a brother, she will kill with as little scruple as Flamineo gave to Marcello's death, and with the same basic sentiments of the embracing of the self that motivate him. If she dies penitent, it is because, contrary to normal belief, she is a rather weaker character than him; who, though, has a trick of cosmetic presentation which Flamineo, despising it in other people, is too honest to use himself.

Yet clearly, what brother and sister both share is a fascination, a total absorption in role-playing. If Flamineo seems almost to go out of his way to provoke both friends and enemies, whereas his sister believes in presenting only her best available face, both continually 'put on an act'.[14] The play is studded with examples from both of them. There is Flamineo pretending to act as go-between to reconcile Vittoria with her husband Camillo, or his pact of melancholia with Lodovico. Vittoria, needing to wriggle out of the predicament she has been placed in by Francisco's cunningly-faked 'love-letter', puts on a wonderful show of 'woman undone' and wronged innocence for the benefit of the jealous Brachiano. In a class of their own are Flamineo's mock-death and Vittoria's magnificent performance in the trial-scene itself. Vittoria performs best in the heroic mode. Her virtue is a mine of diamonds. She will not shed one base tear. She will go limping to heaven on crutches. Flamineo by contrast has a taste for broad farce. His liver is parboiled like Scotch holly-bread. There's a plumber laying pipes in his guts, it scalds. Both are born performers, and performance is a completely natural mode for the solipsist. It confirms the self by making others respond to mere invention. It is often noted how often the principals seem to behave with a strong sense of audience; how, 'in typical scenes we watch actors-watching-actors'; how characters eagerly anticipate the set-pieces – 'Now for two whirlwinds'; how even the choric figures in the play respond not to issues, but to the quality of performance – 'She hath a brave spirit'.[15] It is the perfect theatre for an actor who is playing a character who is putting on an act. The addiction to performance is near-universal. Francisco gives a very striking example with the fake love-letter. He does not simply devise the plan but, even in soliloquy, enjoys it as 'act': 'I am in love,/ In love with Corombona; and my suit/ Thus halts to her in verse'. Intriguingly, this follows a scene with a ghost which anticipates Flamineo's scene in V.iv. with the ghost of Brachiano. The impulse of both men is to question the ghost, and to speculate about the phenomenon of ghosts, rather than to be suitably terrified. Both also rapidly dismiss any thought of ghosts from their minds, and get swiftly down to business. The principal difference with Francisco is that he summons up the ghost in the first place by imagining Isabella's form. The image in his own brain then becomes an independent form, which he interrogates. Yet, immediately, he refuses to let it claim the status of an independent form: 'how idle am I/ To question my own idleness'. He violently removes the ghost from his imagination – 'Out of my brain with't' – and it obediently exits. The effect is as confusing to us as to him. It seems that we *have* seen a ghost.

Yet, earlier in the play, we have already observed two extended dumb-shows, summoned up for Brachiano's benefit by the 'strong-commanding art' of the conjuror (II.ii). The dumb-shows enacted 'real' events, though clearly not simultaneously with their occurrence in 'life'. They are either re-enacted by spirits; or else the conjuror has windows into at least one real time-scale beyond his own. That one would be Isabella's murder: the murder of Camillo is described in the present tense, and the conjuror announces that he and Brachiano had better make a quick escape from Vittoria's house, since guards are already on their way to arrest her in connection with the murder. However, in the case of Isabella, this means that her image has already been summoned up in the play, at will. It is therefore possible that Francisco does exactly the same: summon up by imagination something that has its own reality. Notably, both the conjuror and Francisco speak of fitting the 'act (with) a tragic sound' (II.ii.37), or a 'tragedy . . . (with) idle mirth in't' (IV.i.117), or 'an old wives' story' (IV.i.114). What this means is that to them the imagination seems more significant than that 'own reality'. The imagination creates reality.

In fact, for these characters there is no other reality. It is this which makes manipulators out of all the evil characters, since there is so little sense of the reality of others. Duke Francisco seems to be determined to destroy Brachiano, Vittoria and the rest *because* they killed his beloved sister. Yet, this is an emotion he seems to have to whip up, as he shows in IV.i: 'To fashion my revenge more seriously/ Let me remember my dead sister's face' (96–7). Can we at all trust the idea of his brotherly love, when Zanche confirms that Brachiano did murder Isabella, and Lodovico cries that 'now our action's justified', only for Francisco to reply, 'Tush for justice' (V.iii.264)? What his 'true' motive might be is always obscure. It seems largely to consist of the pleasures of Machiavellianism, both in terms of deviousness and of cruelty. Above all, it consists of his capacity to outsmart other politicians. He takes most pleasure in his plot to send the fake love-letter to Vittoria, knowing that this will provoke a jealous quarrel, a reconciliation and a jail-break (which Brachiano thinks was cleverly plotted). Francisco's delight (IV.iii.52) derives from using another man's cleverness against him. Similarly, he manipulates Lodovico and his own brother, contriving to make Lodovico think that Monticelso (who has just preached against revenge) has paid him to do the murders. Ingenuity is also important in the actual murder devices; and in V.i. he and Lodovico compete in inventing the most original mode of despatching Brachiano. In the end, it seems that what he most commits himself to is not the motive for the act (which seems actually no worthier than Lodovico's recollected lust for Isabella), but the quality of the act itself. That quality is measurable by the extent to which his intelligence can triumph over others, and so assert itself. Francisco and Lodovico constantly flatter themselves that they are committing 'a glorious act' which will immortalize them. For Lodovico, the act confirms his sense of self: 'I do glory yet,/ That I can call this act mine own. For my part,/ The rack, the gallows and the torturing wheel/ Shall be but sound sleeps to me. Here's my rest:/ I limn'd this night-piece and it was my best' (V.vi.293–7). He can die a happy man, having committed a series of exquisite murders; or rather, having created them. His pleasure is that of the artist revelling in his imaginative power. The 'act' he has committed is partly theatrical, but it gives the only available solidity to his existence. As with Flamineo, Lodovico has used the destruction of others to confirm himself.

If he is in his turn killed, this seems not to trouble him. Had he thought of others – which he does not – he might comfort himself with the knowledge that integrity seems something of an impossibility. Innocence not only is despised and destroyed, but also invariably compromises itself.[16] It is not a choice therefore between the solidity of innocence, measured against the 'act' of evil. Good, simply because of its concern for others beyond itself, seems always in the end to abandon its position. Cornelia preaches against the immorality of her eldest children; yet, in the face of their intransigence, she will take Marcello, and follow them to the court, live on their immoral earnings, see her innocent son murdered by his brother, and be driven insane herself. Her last sane act is to insist that Marcello provoked his own death. An anonymous page is especially invented by Webster to contradict her: 'This is not true, Madam' (V.ii.65). More spectacularly, Isabella is drawn not only into lies, but into an entire 'act', by her attempt to reclaim Brachiano's affections.[17] In II.i, she counterfeits all the symptoms of raging jealousy for the benefit of her brothers, so that she will be given the blame for Brachiano's infidelities. She imitates exactly the 'divorce' from Brachiano that Brachiano had earlier spoken to her when they were alone. Unfortunately, her convincing performance is entirely ineffectual. A few lines later, Brachiano is plotting to poison her, and a few lines beyond that, Francisco and Monticelso

are going ahead with their plan to kill Brachiano. She confessedly
plays a part (II.i.224). All that her part achieves is self-compromise.
It certainly achieves no respect. At the end of the touching scene
when Isabella is seen to kiss the picture of her husband before
going to bed, and is therefore by his means poisoned, his only
comment to the Conjuror is, 'Excellent, then she's dead' (II.ii.24).
The value the solipsist puts on his own life is everything. Any value
he concedes to others is merely the trick of his own rhetoric, as
with Flamineo's vastly exaggerated praise of the conjuror (II.i).[18]

The point is that it is innocence, not evil, which in this play
seems to lack a sense of direction. No matter how dislocated the
language of the wicked may be in the play – and it is nothing if
not brilliantly fragmented and aphoristic[19] – the fragments do not
in the end signify a condition of directionlessness. When only the
self matters, words need no longer be used for mere communication
with others. The self nevertheless does still have a purpose, though
the purpose seems to consist of little more than its own self-assertions, and though what confirms the sense of self most incontestibly
is the destruction of others. These self-assertions are shared by all
the evil-doers in the play. What in the end separates Flamineo and
to a lesser extent Vittoria from the rest, is the fact that self-assertion
in their cases turns out to be an act also of exploration. Flamineo
is a true experimenter, pushing back the boundaries of his own
conscience, and pushing towards the ultimate areas of his own
feelings and those of others. Always delighting in exploiting pre-
tences and hypocrisies, his most bizarre experiment – the mock
death – is a means of finding the truth about his sister's feelings.
His most violent experiment – the murder of his brother – is a
means of finding out the truth about his own.

5
The Duchess of Malfi

Webster's second tragedy intriguingly varies the moral experiment: this time he studies pretensions to innocence. But if the Duchess achieves a *de facto* innocence in martyrdom, the good in Bosola is overwhelmed by his moral enquiry.

To the endless self-obsession of the characters of Jacobean drama, *The Duchess of Malfi* seems at first a wholesome exception. It particularly seems so in connection with the theme of family. The unhealthy destruction of all family ties and values seems the norm of all other major Jacobean plays. *The Duchess of Malfi* by contrast seems to set out to celebrate those ties and values.[1] It contains, in the second scene between the Duchess, Antonio, and the maid Cariola (III.ii), a scene of affectionate domestic playfulness unparalleled in the drama of this period. It is a scene which Webster has added to his sources. It is relaxed and playful, containing the kind of mild sexual humour – 'she's the sprawling'st bedfellow' – which only comes from a happy marriage. Antonio is clearly a man who likes women, and who is very good at pleasing them, in every way. He has a sense of the ludicrous, as he shows in his amusing description of the dilemma of Paris ('For how was't possible he could judge right,/ Having three amorous goddesses in view,/ And they stark naked?'). His teasing remarks about 'hard-favour'd ladies' and how they insist on having 'worse-favour'd waiting women' come from a deeply felt confidence in their love and in his own. The silly joke which so horrendously backfires, of he and Cariola sneaking from the room, leaving the Duchess talking to herself, could and should have ended in a great deal of giggling. The scene is so well written, it plays itself; and it sets the theme for everything that follows. It is the only purely playful scene Webster allows the couple, but from this point onwards their domestic roles become an essential part of their presentation, particularly with the Duchess. It is as wife and as mother that she suffers and dies. Causelessly tortured and murdered by a brother, her belief in husband and children remains unbroken. It is a theme which is systematically deployed. The children appear with her at the shrine of Loretto (III.iv) and in the

74

separation scene, engineered by her brothers, which follows it. There, the Duchess, parting from both husband and eldest son, sees her grief in terms of a childish image: 'I have seen my little boy oft scourge his top/ And compar'd myself to't: naught made me e'er/ Go right but Heaven's scourge-stick' (III.v.79–81). Webster readily and insistently uses the Duchess' family as a source of pathos in these scenes. Antonio's farewell to his wife, here, is an example of the typical diminutive mode, with its reference to a 'sweet armful' of children, and its parting plea, 'if I do never see thee more,/ Be a good mother to your little ones,/ And save them from the tiger' (84–6). In the scene of the Duchess' death, the same kind of pathos is the very foundation of her resilience. During her torture, she had not only represented innocent family values, but had been tested in a way which had most cruelly assailed those values: '*Here is discovered, behind a traverse, the artificial figures of Antonio and his children appearing as if they were dead*' (IV.i.55). Yet, in her death scene, the Duchess seems to have penetrated the lie, or to have forgotten it. Her last simple, pathetic instructions to Cariola, regarding the children, carry all the force of a last worldly act before she dedicates herself to her martyrdom:

> I pray thee, look thou giv'st my little boy
> Some syrup for his cold, and let the girl
> Say her prayers, ere she sleep.
> 　　　　　　　　　　　Now what you please –
> What death?
>
> 　　　　　　　　　　　　　　　　(IV.ii.203–6)

The Duchess, then, suffers and defies her tragedy, not as an individual alone, but almost as the representative of normal life and family values. Surely, here if anywhere in Jacobean drama, there is a sense of stable faith?[2]

Yet, studies by Frank Wadsworth into how Webster's contemporaries viewed the remarriage of widows or marriage beneath one's rank, and by Gunnar Boklund into the conflicting attitudes of Webster's sources towards the Duchess, proved decades ago that, at least for the sixteenth century, the available response to the central figure was far from clear cut.[3] Boklund argues that the very conflicts of attitude between various versions of a well-known story probably contributed in large measure to Webster's interest in it.[4]

It may have been, not moral certainty, but ambiguity that he sought. We would be wise, if we seek the meaning the play offers, rather than the one which seems to give most comfort, to register not only the fact that a sainted family is persecuted, but that its haloes nevertheless seem precarious. Clearly, this enquiry must begin with the Duchess herself, and with the self-assumed quality of her martyrdom.

It is little short of astonishing that Webster should be able to give his Duchess any spiritual dimension at all. Earlier in the play, her attitude to religion had been unthinking, or even dismissive. In the impromptu ritual which converts her hasty courtship into vows of marriage – 'I have heard lawyers say, a contract in a chamber/ *Per verba de praesenti* is absolute marriage' (I.i.478–9) – the recognition and blessing of the church seems of negligible significance to her, compared with the urgency of her impulses. Her rhetorical questions, framed in the ecstacy of impatience, show her comtempt: 'What can the church force more? . . . How can the church bind faster?' (488, 491). Her rank demands a sense of public institutions and public obligations. She has none.[5] She appears not to understand such ideas. As late as III.ii, Cariola again guides the reactions of normal morality when she objects to the feigned pilgrimage to Ancona: 'I do not like this jesting with religion'. The Duchess roundly calls her a 'superstitious fool' for her scruples (317, 319).

Yet the Duchess' death is suffused with a religious glow. Persecution converts the unthinking into the self-aware. She assumes her own salvation with such massive assurance that she makes death seem, not a defeat, but a reward. As early as her parting from Antonio, religious phraseology begins to invade her speech: 'in the eternal church, sir,/ I do hope we shall not part thus' (III.v.71–2). It seems churlish to observe that she had little time for the eternal church until now. In the image of 'heaven's scourge-stick' in the same scene, she invokes suffering as a spiritual discipline which now gives a necessary shape and meaning to her fears. Everything then collaborates to confirm her theory that suffering is the way to heaven: that, *'There's no deep valley, but near some great hill'* (144). Of the full extent of Bosola's role in her martyrdom, more will be said later, but the whole of the Duchess' torture contributes to that sense of personal significance, of an almost theatrical eminence, which is her curious route to salvation:

> Duch.   I'll tell thee a miracle –
> I am not mad yet, to my cause of sorrow.

Th'heaven o'er my head seems made of molten brass,
The earth of flaming sulphur, yet I am not mad:
I am acquainted with sad misery,
As the tann'd galley-slave is with his oar;
Necessity makes me suffer constantly,
And custom makes it easy – who do I look like now?
Cari. Like to your picture in the gallery,
A deal of life in show, but none in practice;
Or rather like some reverend monument
Whose ruins are even pitied.
Duch.   Very proper:
And Fortune seems only to have her eyesight
To behold my tragedy.

                                                (IV.ii.23–6)

It is not merely that she sees herself as the very centre and focus
of all suffering. It is that the pictorial, plastic, and theatrical allusions
suggest a sense of self-display in suffering which typifies the
Duchess' demeanour in Act IV. It is with a deliberately monumental
dignity that she forgives her executioners. That is part of the 'performance'. When her splendid conceited speech, 'What would it
pleasure me to have my throat cut/ With diamonds?' (216–17)
becomes too long for the limited attention-span of her audience of
thugs and they start whispering, she cuts her lines and re-estab-
lishes her control, as a performer typically does, with an elegant
off-the-cuff joke: 'I would fain put off my last woman's fault,/ I'd
not be tedious with you'. Even when she consents to present herself
for death, she ensures that the initiative remains hers. She instructs
the executioners in what they are to do: 'Pull, and pull strongly,
for your able strength/ Must pull down heaven upon me'. But
instantly, she stops them again: 'Yet stay; heaven-gates are not so
highly arch'd/ As princes' palaces, they that enter there/Must go
upon their knees'. It is only then that, invoking violent death, she
permits them to strangle her. It is she, not they, who will say when
she is to die. All in all, it is a theatrical *tour de force*.[6] For all her
deliberate casting off of worldly faults, her dedication to last things,
her conscious humility, this is an arrogant meekness. Her pride is
indeed what she struggles to preserve. Her 'spirit of greatness'
which Cariola feared was formerly overwhelmed by her 'spirit of
woman' (Act I, end) now quite clearly triumphs. Cariola had, in
that speech, accused her of a 'fearful madness'. Yet, the madness

both of her own sexuality and of the torture-techniques used on her by her brothers are triumphantly surmounted. Impulsiveness has become the pride to endure. The result has been shrewdly called a 'safe composite stereotype of penitent whore, Virgin majestic in grief, serving mother, and patient and true turtle dove mourning her one love'; and the stereotype is in a sense highly synthetic.[7]

However, it is difficult to agree with Lisa Jardine when she goes on to say that 'strength of purpose is *eroded* into strength of character in adversity'.[8] Webster seems not to invite us to respond to the Duchess' earlier conduct as 'strength of purpose'. On the contrary, everything seems to point towards Cariola's verdict being Webster's own. Even putting aside all the theories about the remarriage of widows, or marriage beneath one's own rank, which might render her suspect to Webster's contemporaries, she tends to arouse the prude in all of us by how she behaves in the early scenes. She had clearly already decided to marry Antonio, and must be aware of his adoration, but her task is to overcome his modest restraint. She does so in a courtship scene which moves from business to bed with remarkable rapidity, and one in which she is entirely responsible for pushing the pace.[9] One small hint from Antonio – his use of the word, 'beauteous' – is sufficient cue for her to steer the conversation to marriage. When Antonio looks like escaping into harmless jokes, she has to become bolder. Making her meaning unmistakably plain, she pushes a wedding-ring on his finger, and so begins a whole series of physical moves. It is very plain that, indeed, 'This is flesh, and blood, sir;/ 'Tis not the figure cut in alabaster/ Kneels at my husband's tomb' (I.i.453–5). She kneels instead with her next husband in the quickest available form of marriage, speaking of her 'violent passions' (445), and condemning herself from her own mouth with a veritable barrage of unconscious 'placing' metaphor: of her secret being like poison; of the temptation of a saucy devil; of buying and selling; of a *quietus est*, or final absolution; of thrusting one's hands in the fire to warm them; or of marriage as a 'Gordian Knot', which – contrary to what she thinks – was not untied, but cut with a sword.[10]

Our subsequent impressions of the Duchess are hardly better than the first. The contraction of dramatic time gives the Duchess an advanced pregnancy between Acts I and II, and two more children between Acts II and III. Her conduct in the next scene with Antonio, a public scene, adds to the impression that she is living her life with recklessness and haste. We now have, to guide our responses, a far more potent commentator than her maid: we have Bosola. The lewdness of his comments about her 'apparent signs of breeding' in II.i and II.ii do not seem unfair in the context of her restlessness, her almost open flirtatiousness with Antonio, or her 'most vulturous eating of the apricocks' (II.ii.2). She behaves injudiciously, and the birth of the child takes place in an atmosphere of panic and blunder, culminating with the dropping of the child's horoscope right at the feet of the enemy agent; and the low comedy of the rumour, invented to explain the general panic in the Duchess' household, of a Swiss thief with a great pistol in his codpiece.

Her subsequent 'stereotype' seems distinctly an improvement on all this. It restores a much needed sense of control and dignity, and it serves her well in adversity. The inability of any other character to die well only enhances our admiration of her success. Cariola, who is strangled in the same scene, dies scratching, biting, pleading and lying, and also dies despised and mocked:

> Cari. I am quick with child.
> Bos.　　　　Why, then,
> (*They strangle* Cariola *and bear her off*)
> Your credit's sav'd.

(IV.ii.254–5)

Other deaths are equally terrible. Notable here is the Cardinal's, a death full of the farcical irony which is so typical of the idiom of Jacobean tragedy. He has explicitly instructed his henchmen not to heed cries in the night. The motive for this is to provide cover while he disposes of the body of the mistress he has just murdered. When he himself is murdered and cries out for help, his friends come out to the balcony to laugh at his 'counterfeiting', and declare, 'I'll see him hang'd, ere I go down to him' (V.v.22). The same kind of ironies are also present in the fate of Ferdinand, whose own dying words spell out the theme of ironic retribution: '*Whether we fall by ambition, blood, or lust,/ Like diamonds, we are cut with our own dust*' (V.v.72–3). His insanity and murder very neatly repay his murder of his sister the Duchess, and his attempt to drive her mad. The retribution these two brothers receive is in marked contrast with the 'Mercy' which the Duchess both dispenses and expects. Mercy is what the Cardinal, in his death-scene, pleads for in vain. It follows that the Duchess alone has any sense of her own spiritual salvation. In V.v, the Cardinal, reading a book, is 'puzzled in a question about hell:/ He says, in hell there's one material fire,/ And yet it shall not burn all men alike./ Lay him by: – how tedious is a guilty conscience!/ When I look into the fish-ponds, in my garden,/ Methinks I see a thing, arm'd with a rake/ That seems to strike at me' (V.v.1–7). In a play where domesticity is such a powerful benign force, this is a vision of the devil, and of his own devilishness, which is all the more dreadful for being so full of domestic detail. With a similar despair, his mistress Julia dies, going 'I know not whither' (V.ii.289), and Bosola, bound on 'another voyage', dies 'in a mist' (V.v.94).

There can be no mistaking the histrionic nature of the Duchess' death, and the pride of her brand of humility. She is, however, granted a precious certainty of her own salvation, and a precious confidence in her own identity, dignity and sanity. She dies unbroken, and in this court that gives her an enormous advantage over all others.

One point, though, must be made. If her death is indeed a kind of award, it must be seen as no more than a purely personal award. It is granted to her alone, for her courage. It seems not to extend beyond her into any defensible scheme of reward and punishment, nor into any kind of influence over the lives of others[11]. The key figures here are Bosola and Antonio, and the most significant speech is the one that ends the play. Delio's closing couplet is:

> *Integrity of life is fame's best friend,*
> *Which nobly, beyond death, shall crown the end.*

The phrase, 'integrity of life' is an allusion to the Horace Ode, 'Integer Vitae',[12] familiar to every Elizabethan schoolboy through the medium of Lyly's Latin grammar. In Shakespeare's *Titus Andronicus*, Chiron recognizes the opening lines of this Ode on a scroll sent by Andronicus, and says, 'O, 'tis a verse in Horace; I know it well:/ I read it in the grammar long ago' (IV.ii.22–3). The Loeb translation of the first half of the Ode reads as follows: 'He who is upright in his way of life and unstained by guilt, needs not Moorish darts nor bow nor quiver loaded with poisoned arrows. . . . For as I was singing of my Lalage and wandering far beyond the boundaries of my farm in the Sabine woods, unarmed and free from care, there fled from me a wolf, a monster'. The virtuous lover, Horace humorously claims, is invulnerable. The wolf flees from his integrity of life. The appropriateness of the Ode to the play is obvious. Even the wolf has its counterpart in Ferdinand's lycanthropy. Delio, however, adapts the Ode to his own moral theme. Integrity of life might not actually drive away the wolf, might not preserve one's own life, but it ensures another kind of survival, the survival of one's good name. 'Integrity of life is *fame's best friend*'. In the same speech, he contrasts the Duchess' fame with her brothers': 'These wretched eminent things/Leave no more fame behind 'em than should one/ Fall in a frost and leave his print in snow;/ As soon as the sun shines, it ever melts, both form, and matter' (V.v.113–17). This seems straightforward enough. Delio seems merely to be assuring us that the Cardinal's dying plea, to be 'laid by, and never thought of' (V.v.90), is likely enough to be respected. Compared with his anonymity, the Duchess is a figure that we will never forget. Yet it seems equally clear that, for this survival in fame to occur, it needs *more* than mere virtue. The final complication is that, however celebrated the Duchess may be, she is still, in another sense, neglected.

Here, Antonio is of great significance. The play's curious structure, with its major figure dying in Act IV, with a very long Act V still to follow, would seem to argue that the final phases of the plot are intended in some way to test the survival-power of the Duchess' influence after her death. Bosola's final speech tells of our lives being 'like dead walls, or vaulted graves,/ That ruin'd, yield no echo' (V.v.97–8). Yet the Duchess' life does literally yield an echo, the Echo of V.iii, in which she tries to warn Antonio against his gauche plan to meet and placate the Cardinal:

> Anto. 'Tis very like my wife's voice.
> Echo.   *Ay, wife's voice.*
> Delio.   Come, let's walk farther from't: –
> I would not have you go to th'cardinal's tonight:
> Do not.
> Echo.   *Do not*
>
>   (V.iii.26–9)

This formidable echo gives the audible lie to Bosola's speech about silent, ruined walls. It seems deliberately designed to do so, since the scene is set in the *ruins* of an ancient abbey. But, if heard, the Echo is ignored. Blindly and fatalistically, Antonio blunders on to his death. The Duchess' influence is powerless to save him from it. Worse, she is incapable of saving for him what for her has been most serviceable: faith. He dies, like the wicked, in despair. With a distinct borrowing from a Gloucester speech in *King Lear*, he concludes:

> In all our quest of greatness,
> Like wanton boys whose pastime is their care,
> We follow after bubbles, blown in th'air.
> Pleasures of life, what is't? only the good hours
> Of an ague; merely a preparative to rest,
> To endure vexation.
>
> (V.iv.64–9)

His dying wish is for his son to 'fly the courts of princes'. His wish is not respected. The conclusion from all this is uncompromising: mere innocence is not enough. For 'integrity of life' to guarantee any kind of survival, it must include some ingredient of personal force, some 'spirit of greatness'; the kind of conviction that makes the Duchess proclaim, 'I am Duchess of Malfi still' (IV.ii.142). (For all her domesticity, this is the only name she is ever given.) Various commentators have pointed out that, contrary to the sources, Webster makes Antonio's character a noble and accomplished one. Though hardly an exciting figure – except evidently to the Duchess – he is, but for being a mere steward, an unimpeachable choice for a husband.[13] His virtue is at least the equal of hers. His innocence makes him incapable of vile plots or low suspicions. He therefore dies wretchedly, in despair. He even, like the wicked, dies ironically, killed in error by Bosola: 'Antonio!/ The man I would have sav'd 'bove mine own life' (V.iv.52–3). In no sense is Antonio 'saved' by his own virtue. More disturbingly still, he is not even saved by any surviving influence of the Duchess.

It seems that the play is on the very brink of suggesting that salvation is a matter of opinion. The Duchess is able to convince herself, by force of personality and histrionic talent, that she is bound for heaven. Her conviction is all that matters. The 'true' destination of her soul is not the play's concern. It suffices that, during her life, she is able to save herself from despair and ignominy, be her self-created vision of an afterlife. Here, this Webster play seems at one with one of the major impulses of Jacobean drama. The Old Duke in *The Revenger's Tragedy* had asked, in his death-throes, 'Is there a hell besides this, villains' (III.v.186)? Webster's own Vittoria, in *The White Devil*, watching the death of her husband, in a sense gave him his reply: 'this place is hell' (V.iii.179). Hell is made by men, in these plays. It seems, in *The Duchess of Malfi*, that the same is true of heaven. What in that play matters is not whether you might deserve salvation, but whether you can give your last moments – and hence your life as a whole – some kind of significance, by the force of your conviction. While she lives, the Duchess has the power not only to uphold what she now chooses to stand for, but to secure the unwitting assistance of others in sustaining it. After her death, it is different. Here one thinks principally of Bosola. The Duchess' influence over him intriguingly fluctuates.

From our first acquaintance with Bosola, we are taught to see him in terms of a mixed potential for good and evil. It is Antonio who first describes him in such terms:

> 'Tis great pity
> He should be thus neglected – I have heard
> He's very valiant: this foul melancholy
> Will poison all his goodness.

> (I.i.74–7)

At the end, Bosola represents himself similarly, as 'an actor in the main of all/ Much 'gainst mine own good nature' (V.v.85–6). Initially, of these two impulses, it is clearly the 'foul melancholy' which predominates. In what he calls his 'meditation', he lavishes on two minor grotesques, Castruccio and the Old Lady, his hatred of life:

> But in our flesh though we bear diseases
> Which have their true names only ta'en from beasts,
> As the most ulcerous wolf and swinish measle;
> Though we are eaten up of lice and worms,
> And though continually we bear about us
> A rotten and dead body, we delight
> To hide it in rich tissue: all our fear –
> Nay, all our terror – is lest our physician
> Should put us in the ground, to be made sweet.

> (II.i.52–60)

His second meditation on the same theme seems superficially similar. This time, however, the emphasis vitally shifts from a negative hatred, with nothing to relieve it, to a traditional contempt for the world in the face of an eternity to come:

> What's this flesh? a little crudded
> milk, fantastical puff-paste; our bodies are weaker
> than those paper prisons boys use to keep flies in;
> more contemptible, since ours is to preserve earth-
> worms. Didst thou ever see a lark in a cage? such
> is the soul in the body: this world is her little
> turf of grass, and the heaven o'er our heads, like
> her looking-glass, only gives us a miserable
> knowledge of the small compass of our prison.
>
> (IV.ii.125–33)

The speech comes from the scene where Bosola superintends the Duchess' death. For all that he fulfils without hesitation his brutal commission, it indicates the extent to which, in his successive pretended roles of her tomb-maker and bellman, his function is curiously priestlike. He brings her, as he puts it himself, 'by degrees to mortification' (IV.ii.177). He tunes and adjusts her course to her personal salvation. At one point he corrects despair:

> Duch.   I could curse the stars . . .
> Bos. Look you, the stars shine still.
>
> (IV.i.96–100)

At another, he provides an obvious prompt for her to show her courage in the face of death:

> Bos. Come, be of comfort, I will save your life.
> Duch. Indeed, I have not the leisure to tend so small
> a business.
>
> (IV.i.86–7)

Early in the play, Bosola sees in the pregnant Duchess only an opportunity for his prurient imagination. Here in her death scene, he seems increasingly fascinated by the spectacle of innocence that she performs for him. There is no mistaking the growing intensity with which he treats her.

It seems then that in helping her to die well, Bosola does indeed live up to the ambiguity we expect from his character. He is employed in a villainous office, but discharges that office virtuously. After her death, however, the ambiguity is reversed. He seeks to reform his life and to atone for his crimes, but his good intentions bring only evil. He murders, in error, the Duchess' husband. Puzzlingly, he seems almost deliberately to ensure Antonio's final despair by so baldly telling him that his wife and children were all murdered: it is a strong contrast with the way he comforted the Duchess' last moments by pretending that her children survived. Then, he kills off the two brothers in a 'most just revenge'. We cannot regret their deaths. Yet, in a man who claims, in the same breath as the one that vows their deaths, that, 'still methinks the duchess/ Haunts me' (V.ii.345–6), it seems a strange way to perpetuate her memory. Her last word is 'Mercy', but the quality seems to die with her. The only truly necessary revenge was the one she had already carried out herself, as her dead eyes gazed at Ferdinand and drove him mad: 'Cover her face: mine eyes dazzle: she died young' (IV.ii.264). Yet Bosola, invoking her name, commits himself to the evil that revenge necessarily entails, and dies suspecting himself to be damned. It would seem that, if the Duchess has haunted him, she has haunted him in vain – just as was the case with Antonio. It is not hers, but the influence of Ferdinand, 'rotten, and rotting others' (III.v.19), which claims him. Once again, in the abrupt decline of her influence from the moment of her death, the play casts doubt on the survival-power of her virtue.[14]

The doubt is particularly notable, since it is precisely from the Duchess' death-scenes that the figure of Bosola increasingly takes over the play. His character is, like hers, ambiguous; and his fate is, like hers, self-made. But while he claims to commit that fate to the cause of defensible values, what he seems increasingly to be is a moral experimenter, differing only from other similar figures in other plays by his self-ignorance. He persuades himself that he acts only for the best, but what he does, right to the end, is to use the pretence of loyalty as his warrant to destroy.[15] In Ferdinand's name, he kills the Duchess. In the Duchess' name, he kills Ferdinand (and his brother the Cardinal). In Antonio's name he kills Antonio himself, and destroys his faith. In effect, Webster has intriguingly varied the type. He studies how the key motive of experiment can be found in a less confessedly nihilistic figure than, say, Flamineo; how it can be found, indeed, in a character who believes himself to be a good man, misused by the world. Webster works his way into this theme by first observing, through the highly sympathetic figure of the Duchess, how a similarly unaware character can very successfully edit her moral nature. Once we begin to interpret Bosola as an experimenter, all our observations about his positive influence on the Duchess' fate must be reinterpreted. The focus of such a reinterpretation must be his professed pity for her, in and after the murder scenes.

At the beginning of these scenes, Bosola still appears to her in his own person. By the time of the 'murder' of her children, this establishes him as an enemy. Subsequently, he appears in the more neutral roles of bell-man and tomb-maker. His purpose is only ostensibly to bring comfort. Actually, he is preparing the next useful means of observing a human mind *in extremis*. In a rare moment of perception, Ferdinand sees this: 'Thy pity is nothing of kin to thee' (IV.i.138). The 'pity' is rather the means of enquiry. The known and established pitiless figure of 'Bosola' would have complicated and therefore marred the experiment. In an interesting pun, Bosola claims that his own shape is 'forfeited by [his] intelligence' (135). On the face of it, the word 'intelligence' simply refers to Bosola's established role of spy; or to his (treacherous) dealings with the Duchess. These things would cost him all credibility with her, were he now to appear before her in his own form. Used in this way, 'intelligence' is one of the commoner words in the play, occurring (together with 'intelligencer' and 'intelligency') nine times in all. However, the word can clearly also mean brain-power or acuity or wit. If taken this way, Bosola is claiming that he can no longer use his own identity, because it is in some sense compromised by his cleverness. One shape, one indivisible identity (intriguingly, another term for this would be the 'integrity [wholeness] of life' that Delio praises at the end of the play), is incompatible with the kind of enquiry that now interests him. Bosola has little respect for 'intelligence' in any other sense. He may seem to relish his employment as mere spy, but calls it the 'base quality/ Of intelligencer' (III.ii.327–8). What he rather covets is 'to gain the name of a speculative man' (III.iii.47).[16] Indeed, he now wants more than the name. Certainly, Bosola's University studies, as Delio describes them, were nothing if not bizarre: 'like such who study to know how many knots was in Hercules' club, of what colour Achilles' beard was, or whether Hector were not troubled by the toothache' (42–4). Such a taste for bizarre scholarship may be recognized as one of the possible preliminaries in a quest for moral knowledge which is equally arcane. As he now adopts disguise for the first time in the play, Bosola prepares to discover what happens at a murder.

In doing so, his role will be intriguingly at odds with his commission. He decides to pose in the impersonal roles of bell-man and tombmaker, bringing the Duchess by degrees to mortification; but it is as if he does so only for a better vantage-point. His basic sympathies seem untouched. One proof of this lies in the contrast between his attitude to the Duchess' death and those of her maid and children. His mockery of Cariola's pleas for life has already been mentioned. With the children, he is still more brutal, giving the order for their deaths in the throwaway comment, 'some other strangle the children' (IV.ii.239). This, in a play which seems dedicated to the ideal of family. With the Duchess herself, however, he uses his disguise to give him a kind of impassive distance from his commission. He invents a meditation, a macabre joke, and a funeral dirge, apparently to distract the Duchess and calm her. Nevertheless, he also continues to produce small pieces of deadlier knowledge: the coffin sent by her brothers, the fact that this room is to be her last presence chamber, the nature of the death she is to die. Having fortified her against death, but still reminding her that her death is immediately to come, he then quizzes her: 'Doth not death fright you? . . . Yet, methinks,/ The manner of your death should much afflict you' (IV.ii.210, 213–14). He listens to her final magnificent speeches and watches her being strangled, with no further intervention. Having set up a test of courage, he watches it run its course, and it really seems as if curiosity is far more prominent than pity. Pity is again his means of taunting Ferdinand when the murders have been done, and it is hard to miss the contrast between his order in the murder scene, 'some other strangle the children', and his display of pity now, for Ferdinand's benefit:

> But here begin your pity –
> *[Shows the Children strangled]*
> Alas, how have these offended?

> (IV.ii.257–8)

The ploy does not immediately work, so Bosola draws Ferdinand's attention to the Duchess herself. Here, he draws blood, as his employer experiences the full realization that he has destroyed his sister. Bosola then chooses this moment to clamour for payment. His claims are of interest partly because of the gloss he places on his own reasons for committing such a crime: 'I serv'd your tyranny, and rather strove/ To satisfy yourself than all the world;/ And though I loath'd the evil, yet I lov'd/ You that did counsel it; and rather sought/ To appear a true servant than an honest man' (IV.ii.329–33). His reason, then, was misplaced loyalty, overruling his true principles. He now repents. However, the very first mention of a 'sweet and golden dream' (324) betrays at least one motive beyond previous loyalty and present guilt. He killed for money. Our acceptance of the idea that he now feels guilt or tenderness for the Duchess must contend against the knowledge that he still wants to be well paid for murdering her, and will if necessary kill again to get his money.

The idea of Bosola's pity or conscience immediately undergoes a still stiffer test. Ferdinand leaves, and Bosola soliloquises: 'I would not change my peace of conscience/ For all the wealth in Europe' (340–1). At this point, the Duchess momentarily revives! Bosola goes into a frenzy of concern to save her. After all, his own soul hangs on the issue: 'Her eye opes,/ And heaven in it seems to ope, that late was shut' (347–8). Not daring to call for help, he tries to keep her alive with frantic lies about the survival of her family. When he fails, he weeps with frustration, and then seems amazed by his own tears: they 'never grew/ In my mother's milk' (362–3). It is, however, precisely at the moment of this baptism in feeling that he vows to do something 'worth *my* dejection' (375). The astounding return to money and self, here, confirms that his later revenges, committed in the Duchess' name, might just as plausibly stem from pique at a rejected pay-claim.

Bosola later wonders why his 'penitent fountains' were 'frozen up' while the Duchess was still living. Presumably, they were dried by his own curiosity. They flow now in a kind of post-experimental depression, which lasts for the rest of the play. Actually, unlike Flamineo in the earlier Webster tragedy, Bosola has few people at all on whom he can experiment, being apparently without family. With the Duchess dead, and especially after his accidental killing of Antonio, he has even fewer. Increasingly, his only obvious targets are Ferdinand and the Cardinal. But, more than that, the ultimate experiment seems to be on himself. His mission to the Cardinal's palace actually seems to make nonsense of the idea that his 'real' motive is financial.[17] Rather, he seems bent on making another enemy, which will precipitate some crisis in his own life:[18]

> Oh, my fate moves swift!
> I have this cardinal in the forge already,
> Now I'll bring him to th'hammer . . .
> I will not imitate things glorious,
> No more than base; I'll be mine own example.
>
> (V.iv.78–82)

The ostensible subject of his determination is to 'hammer' the cardinal. However, this subject is crowded out by other thoughts which are far more self-obsessed. It is his own fate which preoccupies him: unsurprisingly, since he clearly now expects imminent death. He wants to ensure that his fate is 'original': imitative of neither the glorious nor the base deeds of others. In the event, he very imperfectly borrows from several modes: the avenger, the malcontent and the man of integrity. All these roles are jumbled together in his last speeches. He egotistically glories in the overthrow of the mighty Cardinal; but then sees himself as cleansing his life by a final allegiance to a just cause; only to lapse once again into complaint of financial neglect. He dies unsure whether he has earned the peace of 'so good a quarrel', or whether his is 'another voyage'. With eight killings to his name, it is a reasonable doubt. It is only surprising that he has any illusions of final innocence. There is no doubt that he does have good in him. That is precisely what lends fascination to the spectacle of him setting out, like other far more cynical experimenters, to see how far he can violate his own goodness; what evil he can achieve; and what will happen to him when he does so. Like all the other experimenters, he is also irresistibly drawn to tamper with the fates of others, and see how they live and die.[19] Again like the others, at some stage or another in their career, he discovers an exhilarating existential freedom in his own acts of violation. The only difference is in the degree of confusion he suffers as to his own motives and identity. He insists on believing that it is someone else's fault if he becomes 'an actor in the main of all/ Much 'gainst mine own good nature' (V.v.85–6), and never comes anywhere near the recognition that his own chief motives are experimental. Believing, apparently, in each in turn of his own assumed and contradictory roles, his career is nevertheless a whole series of tricks to discover things. He feels he must gain knowledge, or '[his] intelligence will freeze else' (II.iii.6). His life has become a moral experiment, even though an unconscious one; and all the best proof of this comes from the passages where he apparently believes he is acting for the best.

With a twin focus, the play takes one ambiguous figure – the Duchess – and observes her self-created martyrdom. It takes the other ambiguous figure – Bosola – and observes his moral self-destruction as he experiments with evil. Both processes are self-made, and neither character is remotely aware of that fact. In effect, neither realises that his or her prized innocence is a kind of masquerade, and this makes any strong moral preference between them precarious, however tempting. It is the play's most intriguing area of enquiry.

6

'Tis Pity She's a Whore

Even on the most partial computation, by accepting the earliest possible date of composition for the play, or by reading the dedication's reference to 'these first fruits of my leisure' as meaning that the play was Ford's first independent work, *'Tis Pity She's a Whore* is still not quite a Jacobean tragedy. Very possibly, it was written considerably later, perhaps as late as its year of publication, 1633. Only, therefore, with some degree of special pleading can the play find any place in a book on Jacobean drama.

This, however, has always been one of the minor problems that Ford poses. His major plays come as much as a decade after the last major tragedies of the Jacobean era (Middleton's). They arrive as if out of a void, or at least after a particularly barren decade for good tragedy, the 1620s. They are contemporaneous with those of a quite new and distinct group of Caroline playwrights: Glapthorne, Davenant, Killigrew. Yet, on the other hand, his date of birth (1586), his frequent borrowings from Elizabethan and Jacobean authors, his earlier collaborations with Middleton, Dekker, Rowley, Webster et al., seem to argue that his essential affiliations are with an earlier period. We are faced with the choice of observing pure chronology, and taking him as a Caroline dramatist, or of respecting the higher chronology of where he seems genuinely to belong in dramatic history. For most studies of the drama of the Jacobean period, Ford, and particularly *'Tis Pity She's a Whore*, are simply too good to miss. Certainly, for this study, whatever the oddity of Ford's extreme chronological isolation from the pioneers of moral experiment in Jacobean drama, his work, in *'Tis Pity She's a Whore* is essentially akin to theirs.[1] There is actually no disguised duke here, no chastity test, no readily identifiable 'experiment'. At the same time, the hero's whole career is a quest for moral limits, and he has his author's clear sanction in seeking them.

Giovanni's status as explorer is clear from the first scene, especially in the persistent association of him with the concept of 'wit'. His former University tutor, the Friar, had been so captivated with Giovanni's talents, which were 'A wonder of thine age, throughout

Bononia. . . . How did the University applaud/ Thy government,
behaviour, learning, speech,/ Sweetness, and all that could make
up a man', that he, the Friar, was 'proud of [his] tutelage, and
chose/ Rather to leave [his] books than part with thee' (I.i.49–54).
The problem is the irreligious uses to which Giovanni has put his
intellect since then. The former student 'miracle of wit' (I.i.47) now
seems like other 'wits that presum'd/ On wit too much, by striving
how to prove/ There was no God, with foolish grounds of art'
(I.i.4–6).

The word is always an unstable one, particularly in Ford's century.
Capable of meaning the faculty of understanding, or the capacity
of intellect, or the man of high intellectual achievement, it can also
mean mere mental dexterity, the power to amuse, or the man whose
life proves his intelligent and possibly nihilistic frivolity. As the
seventeenth century wears on, the second meaning comes to pre-
dominate over the first, to the point where one indignant writer
refers to 'a kind of sublimated wits that will own neither God nor
Devil'. Ford's use of the word seems to vacillate. He uses the word
in speaking of Giovanni's virtues as a 'miracle of wit', or conversely
in measuring, say, the idiot Bergetto's failings: 'why, thou great
baby, wilt never have wit?' (I.iii.46). He uses it to describe Donado's
exercise of diplomacy on behalf of the same Bergetto, his nephew:
'Once in my time I'll set my wits to school' (83). Most interesting
of all is the word's usage in the long 'seduction' scene of Annabella
by her brother. He tells her that he has obeyed the Friar's instructions, prayed, fasted, and wept, in his attempt to suppress his
desire for her: 'what wit or art/ Could counsel, I have practic'd'
(I.ii.149–50). The distinction is actually a little obscure. Of the three
activities, praying, fasting and weeping, which is 'wit' and which
is 'art'? Or are all three 'wit' or 'art', to be set against other
unspecified mortifications, which are 'art' or 'wit'? Possibly, 'wit'
here signifies some spontaneous exercise of the mind's higher powers, whilst 'art' describes some more calculated performance. In
this case, 'wit' may refer to prayer and weeping; 'art' to fasting. If
so, 'wit' here takes on its most idealistic form in the play.

On the other hand, it is also used to describe Giovanni's shortcom-
ings, ('presum[ing] on wit too much'), or as a synonymn for other
characters' worldliness: the Cardinal's, for instance, when he tells
those who vainly demand that he yield up his fellow-Roman and
fellow aristocrat, the murderer Grimaldi, 'learn more wit, for shame'
(II.ix.59). The word is again used in connection with abrasive cyni-

cism when Giovanni's sister, Annabella, rebuffs her suitor Soranzo so mercilessly (she is already her brother's mistress) that he begs her to 'leave those fruitless strifes of wit' (III.ii.30). In this sense, 'wit' takes its place alongside other words in the play such as 'cunning' (II.i.77) or 'wise' (II.ii.135) which denote unscrupulousness.

Prolific in the first half of the play, the word entirely dies out in Acts IV and V, seeming to signify that Ford was trying to establish something early on, by its use. If any path can be picked between the contradictions, it is that 'wit' is a natural intellectual endowment, enjoyed little by some, and richly by others. At its best, it seems associated with the highest spiritual gifts of a man. It can nevertheless be put to other uses; crueller, and more exploitative. The interesting thing is that not only can wit be put to either more or less innocent uses; it can also be used either more or less innocently; and the two things are not necessarily synonymous.

To be more explicit: when we hear of Giovanni having first come to attention as an outstandingly brilliant young scholar, we understand that he had distinguished himself not only by the completely spontaneous exercise of his gifts, but also by the singular virtue with which he had deployed them: in both ways, his 'wit' had been used innocently. At the extreme opposite end of the scale, when the Cardinal seems to shield a murderer from justice for purely worldly motives, his wit is used for corrupt ends, and he knowingly uses it thus: in neither way is his 'wit' innocent. A third extreme possibility is provided by the wholly innocent idiot, Bergetto, as harmless as he is witless. A fourth permutation is defined by Giovanni as he actually appears in the play, and by his sister Annabella. They apparently exercise their intelligence to corrupted ends; yet perhaps do so innocently or unknowingly.

It is this most complex of the four possibilities that interests Ford. The implication is that he is willing to explore the possible existence of a kind of moral innocence unconnected with the traditional ethical qualities assigned to certain activities. It is a possibility that he is prepared to test to the utmost; as he proves, by choosing actions which have always attracted the utmost repugnance and the strongest of taboos. By making incest his subject-matter, and by exploring the very possibility that it could be seen as in any way innocent, Ford signals his interest in exploring the relativity of even apparently absolute moral standards. He is in other words interested in moral experiment, and Giovanni must therefore be interpreted as a moral explorer on his author's behalf.[2]

It must be confessed, however, that the experiment gets off to a most unpromising start. Ford begins by giving incest a poor press, both in the behaviour of the lovers themselves, the nature of their 'enemies', and the nature of their friends.

If we begin with their 'enemies', it is clear that the play at least begins with a domestic situation which is extremely benign. Neither Giovanni nor his sister could plead any kind of martyrdom. On the contrary, they seem blessed with a father, Florio, who is a model of humanity. He has a most marriageable daughter, and there are three wealthy offers for her. The offer most immediately on hand is from Donado, the 'rich magnifico' (I.ii.118), who wishes to match her with his idiot nephew Bergetto. Here, however, is the answer he receives from Florio:

> Signior Donado, you have said enough,
> I understand you; but would have you know
> I will not force my daughter 'gainst her will.
> You see I have but two, a son and her;
> And he so devoted to his book,
> As I must tell you true, I doubt his health:
> Should he miscarry, all my hopes rely
> Upon my girl; as for worldly fortune,
> I am, I thank my stars, blest with enough.
> My care is how to match her to her liking:
> I would not have her marry wealth, but love,
> And if she like your nephew, let him have her,
> Here's all that I can say
>
> (I.iii.1–13)

In an age in which that great champion of civil liberty, the lawyer Sir Edward Coke, took his daughter (who happened not to agree with his choice of her future husband), tied her to the bedpost, and beat her until she submitted, Florio seems anything but a tryant to his children. What is more, his insistence that his daughter be allowed to marry for love is not only laudable in itself, but is given considerable poignancy by its context. We hear this speech immediately after Giovanni has seduced Annabella. We already know that it was not his scholarly zeal but his sexual frustration that had wasted his body, and that the daughter Florio's care, is lavished on, is at the moment perhaps in bed with her brother.

She is, in a particularly ironic way, already 'matched to her liking'. In short, it is a speech which makes the incestuous lovers look bad. It is only later that Florio becomes more insistent that Soranzo would make a most suitable husband for Annabella. As soon as he does so, the change has some positive impact on the lovers. For the moment, though, his generosity seems to smear them with something of the shame of a major betrayal, and he sustains it despite Donado's extremely handsome offers to endow a marriage of Annabella to Bergetto with great wealth. When, later, Annabella frankly confesses that she will not have Bergetto, Donado, too, seems willing to act nobly:

> Why, here's plain dealing, I commend thee for't,
> And all the worst I wish thee is, Heaven bless thee!
> Your father yet and I will still be friends,
> Shall we not, Signior Florio?
>
> (II.vi.54–7)

Florio's reply, 'Yes, why not?' seems particularly modern in tone, but certainly reflects the matter-of-fact plainness of an uncomplicated man, and Donado sustains the sense of generosity by rewarding Annabella's rejection of his nephew with the gift of a jewel to bless whatever marriage she did accept. We seem to be watching a social group which is probably as wealthy as any group of courtiers, but pleasingly free of the kind of warped arrogance that so often marks them in the drama of this period. It seems a solid, sane and generous world. The only aberrant beings in it are the play's hero and heroine.

This is an impression which Giovanni and Annabella do much to encourage, initially. This seems true especially of Giovanni's mental capacities. He gives little proof in the vital first scene with the Friar of the genius which had once stunned a whole University.[3] His first speech betrays the belief, puerile enough in our own century, let alone his, that the very act of 'coming out of the closet' entitles him to practise his aberrations, at will: 'Gentle father,/ To you I have unclasp'd my burdened soul. . . And yet is here the comfort I shall have,/ Must I not do what all men else may, love?' He goes on to argue that closeness of kinship is all the greater reason for closeness of sexual affection: a concept which could just as conveniently be used to justify any kind of philoprogenitive

perversion. When he responds to the Friar's wholesome recommen-
dation of repentance and contrition with, 'O do not speak of that,
dear confessor', we cannot but agree with his former tutor's disbe-
lieving question, 'Art thou, my son, that miracle of wit/ Who once,
within these three months, wert esteem'd/ A wonder of thine age?'
(I.i.47–9). Certainly, Giovanni gives little proof of it now. When he
exits, promising to try fasting and praying in order to 'free [him]
from the rod/ Of vengeance' (83–4), but insisting that if he still feels
the same as before he'll declare his fate his god, it is difficult to
withhold judgement on his stupidity. The inefficacy of such prayers
would not usually be grounds for atheism; and if, on the other
hand, God does really exist, He would be most unusually clement
to accept so meagre a peace offering.

In his next appearance, he seems to believe that he is propelled
only by fate, not at all by lust (I.ii.154), even though his language
is of the 'hidden flames/ That have almost consum'd [him]' (218–19).
He repeats to Annabella the ridiculous argument that their proximity of birth demonstrates that Nature meant them for each other.
Finally, he lies to her:

> I have ask'd counsel of the holy church,
> Who tells me I may love you, and 'tis just
> That since I may, I should; and will, yes will:
>
> (237–9)

The lie is effective, and moments later, they are vowing, ominously,
'Love me or kill me', before going to bed. It is this scene which is
immediately followed by the one between his father, and Donado,
and the juxaposition with the old men's well-meaning innocence
does not necessarily favour the lovers. In our times, we have seen
adolescents experimenting dangerously in areas utterly bewildering
to their parents. One can only guess at the shock-effect of this plot
of incest, three-and-a-half centuries ago, in the light of what we
understand of their expectations of what a good son and daughter
should be. Certainly, though, we can understand that Florio's own
pride in his son and daughter, and his concern for them, could
hardly be answered with a more violent irony; an irony clearly
intended by the sequence of the two scenes, and the father's unconscious talk of 'miscarriage' and of matching his daughter to her
liking.

The lovers' case is hardly improved by the one clear and unequivocal ally they have: the nurse, Putana. One expects, of course, a little worldliness from a nurse. Certainly we expect this nurse to comment freely on her mistress' suitors, and perhaps, since she has been well-bribed, urge her mistress to a preference for one. Putana does not here disappoint us. She strongly recommends Soranzo, who, despite his well-known adultery with Hippolita, is at least reputed to be undiseased, even at the age of twenty-three (I.ii.85–95). However, Putana's worldiness seems specifically designed to exceed the norms.[4]

She is present when Annabella emerges from her first night with her brother, and greets her mistress with the expected smutty comments. These, though, include the following proposition:

> Your brother's a man,
> I hope, and I say still, if a young wench feel the fit upon her,
> let her take anybody, father or brother, all is one.

(II.i.47–9)

The nurse is clearly in her way a comic character, but the comedy is dangerous to our sympathies for the lovers. Here, in particular, it reduces to the absurd Giovanni's favourite argument, that proximity of blood is the best reason for incest: sister, brother, mother, grandfather, what's the difference? The beauty of the idea rather wilts under such specific imaginings. Once again, the next character to enter is the loving parent, Florio, and once again his speeches generate a pathetic irony, as he speaks, for instance, of how his daughter Annabella 'hath not quite forgot/ To touch an instrument' (78–9).

If the incestuous lovers survive such an introduction, it is presumably because Ford deliberately rescues them. It does indeed seem as if he initially gives them the most hostile of introductions, and then sets out to redeem them, almost as a kind of self-imposed challenge. Once again, our attitudes and sympathies are as much conditioned by those who surround the lovers as by Giovanni and Annabella themselves. Actually, this seems very deliberate, since the lovers are about to enter a dormant phase, while various other characters are introduced.

Prominent among them is the suitor whom her father now increasingly begins to press her to accept: Soranzo. Seen for the first time in the long second scene of the second act, Soranzo at first seems to be a most idealistic lover.[5] He speaks scathingly of how Annabella's beauties far surpass that of the sonneteers' mistresses, and what genius his beloved would have inspired, had the poets only seen her. His encomium is, however, interrupted by another character. It is here that Putana's reference to an affair with the married woman, Hippolita, intrudes with devastating force. Ford makes sure, here, that Soranzo is not condemned for his past record with this woman, but rather for his treatment of her here and now.

The now cast-off Hippolita soon specifies his past treacheries. Apparently, he swore, 'whilst yet [her] husband liv'd,/ That [he would] wish no happiness on earth/ More than to call [her] wife' (68–70). This in itself is so familiar a line of seduction that we might perhaps condemn Soranzo for nothing more serious than use of cliché. What Hippolita, believing him literally, then proceeded to do was entirely on her own initiative. She pressed her husband to undertake a dangerous voyage to Leghorn, to rescue an orphaned niece; hoping that he would die in the journey. Apparently, he did so.

No doubt the hypothetical situation intrigued Ford's trained lawyer's mind, and her putative guilt of murder might exercise a court's intelligence even today. Certainly, her willingness to commit a crime of passion is confirmed by her resolve, now, to plot Soranzo's own death for deserting her. Yet, this is not the real issue. What emerges most strikingly from this scene is not Hippolita's guilt but Soranzo's self-righteousness. He must know the extent to which he inflamed this woman. If he never incited her to murder her husband, he nevertheless seduced her from her husband with his promises, and might feel some twinge of responsibility for her 'crime', the guilt of which clearly haunts her (to her credit). In fact, Hippolita's husband Richardetto was not killed in the voyage to Leghorn. He haunts the play in disguise, now, seeking revenge: and the revenge he seeks is not against his wife but against Soranzo. This in itself is some small signal of Soranzo's shared guilt in Hippolita's offences. At the very least, knowing that the passion he enjoyed in her has now disgraced her, 'And how the common voice allows thereof' (II.iii.13), Soranzo might feel some sympathy. He is more interested, however, in improvising an ingenious new moral rule to exonerate himself:

> The vows I made you, if you remember well,
> Were wicked and unlawful: 'twere more sin
> To keep them than to break them.
>
> (84-6)

As to his partial responsibility for her husband's death:

> think thou
> How much thou hast digress'd from honest shame
> In bringing of a gentleman to death
> Who was thy husband, such a one as he,
> So noble in his quality, condition,
> Learning, behaviour, entertainment, love,
> As Parma could not show a braver man.
>
> (87-93)

These virtues of Hippolita's husband had apparently not occurred to Soranzo when he was seducing her. Now, however, he remembers her husband as a paragon. He urges her,

> Learn to repent and die, for by my honor
> I hate thee and thy lust: you have been too foul.
>
> (98-9)

Ford produces here a splendid comic caricature of a sanctimonious hypocrite, and he produces the portrait within seconds of the first appearance of this vital character. So much depends on our sympathy or otherwise for Soranzo. He is in both senses injured by Giovanni, who so outrageously anticipates him not only in love but in revenge. He is laughed at by both lovers (openly so by Annabella) and used by both of them as the convenient cover of married respectability for Annabella's incestuous pregnancy. If remotely he might seem to emerge in the play as the wronged romantic hero, there would be no question of our feeling anything but repugnance for the lovers. The scene with Hippolita is crucial as early conditioning, in ensuring that this is not the case. If, later, Soranzo cries out against the injustice of being cuckolded and deceived, we cannot but experience some sense of poetic justice at the fate of a man who corrupts and deserts another man's wife, but expects nothing but virtue in his own.

We therefore might feel some qualms about the way, on the failure of Hippolita's scheme of revenge against Soranzo, the pious chorus of onlookers comments on the righteousness of heaven, and its 'wonderful justice', and on how richly deserved an end the 'vile creature' Hippolita has come to: 'Here's the end/ Of lust and pride' (IV.i.88–102). Whatever Hippolita's most recent crimes, the verdict seems too heavily to weight the verdict in Soranzo's favour. He goes on to earn our further displeasure at his evident cowardice. Wife-battering may not, by Jacobean standards, be proof of this by itself, though such scenes are rare enough in the drama of the period to carry a certain shock value when they do occur. The precise amount of violence seems very much to be at the director's discretion. The text mentions only dragging her and pulling her about by the hair. Nevertheless, Vasques, when he interrupts the scene, sees Annabella as being in danger of her life, and protests – perhaps disingenuously – "twere most unmanlike' (IV.iii.81). Later, when Soranzo discovers the identity of Annabella's lover, and plans his death, it is not face to face, but with the aid of a somewhat preposterous gang of banditti, into whose trap he lures Giovanni with smiles and courtesy. The smiling revenger is no stranger to Jacobean drama, but most prefer to administer their brand of justice by their own hand. But then, we had already seen him, at the beginning of the play, instructing his servant Vasques to stab Grimaldi, a rival suitor for Annabella; protesting that he himself could not stoop to take arms in person against so base a fellow (I.ii.42). His excuse for not fighting would have been transparently cowardly to an age well used to private quarrels in the streets on the most trivial of causes: especially since Grimaldi is more than Soranzo's equal in blood, being 'nobly born;/ Of princes' blood' (III.ix.55–6). Incidentally, Grimaldi compounds the impression of the ignobility of the normal world, by trying in return to ambush Soranzo in the dark with a poisoned sword and then hiding behind the skirts of the Cardinal, his fellow-Roman.

As ever, established Catholic religion receives an unsympathetic showing. Ford's Cardinal is actually far less culpable than many of his counterparts in Jacobean drama. He is certainly no murderer. However, he is certainly a snob, and his sense of justice is heavily partial to other Romans, his fellow-townsmen. The immediate protection he extends to the murderer Grimaldi is made to seem particularly repugnant by its sneering tone:

> I here receive Grimaldi
> Into his holiness' protection.
> He is no common man, but nobly born;
> Of princes' blood, though you, Sir Florio,
> Thought him too mean a husband for your daughter.
> If more you seek for, you must go to Rome,
> For he shall thither; learn more wit, for shame.
> Bury your dead – Away, Grimaldi – leave 'em.

(III.ix.53–60)

However, if the Cardinal is a cynic, the Friar at least surely is a good man? Consistently, he seems to exert himself to rescue Giovanni; and if he is unsuccessful here, he has better fortune with Annabella. To her, he delivers a model sermon on the pains of hell for sinners, aptly concentrating on the pangs of the incestuous. Given that Florio has now abruptly become far less tolerant of his daughter's coyness, and far more insistent on her marrying Soranzo, it is hardly surprising that Annabella attends, finally, to the Friar's counsel. In a sense, therefore, he can boast a major success, in reclaiming her from damnation, and reminding her that she must 'despair not; Heaven is merciful' (III.vi.34). True, after her marriage to Soranzo, she suffers a considerable spiritual lapse when her pregnancy is detected, and when she so defiantly throws all her former sins in her husband's face. Nevertheless, she has regained her spiritual composure by the very next scene after that (V.i). Restored to the balcony from which her virtue fell in Act I, she sighs her penitence, her conviction that it is virtue rather than beauty which should be valued, and her fears for her brother's soul. She longs for the guidance once again of 'that man, that blessed friar,/ Who...told me oft/ I trod the path to death, and showed me how' (V.i.24–7). As if providentially, the friar is below, to witness her purity and to catch the letter of warning to her brother, which she throws randomly down in hope of its finding its way to him:

> FRIAR   Lady, Heaven hath heard you,
> And hath by providence ordain'd that I
> Should be his minister for your behoof.

Duly, in her subsequent death scene (V.v), Annabella's mouth is
full of the language which the Friar had implanted: of heaven, of
angels, and of forgiveness.

However, this is the full extent of the Friar's success. He is no
more able to avert the lovers' catastrophe than he was to prevent
their union. This in itself could be largely blamed on Giovanni's
stubbornness, were it not for the suggestions of weakness that
attach to the Friar himself. In this connection, his final speech to
Giovanni is worth quoting entire:

> Go where thou wilt; I see
> The wildness of thy fate draws to an end,
> To a bad fearful end. I must not stay
> To know thy fall; back to Bononia I
> With speed will haste, and shun this coming blow.
> Parma, farewell; would I had never known thee,
> Or aught of thine! Well, young man, since no prayer
> Can make thee safe, I leave thee to despair.

> (V.iii.63–70)

It is a speech which marks the Friar's final transition from hand-
wringing to hand-washing. It is notable not for its fine rhetorical
skills, but for its tendency to retreat in to the commonplaces of all
scenes of recrimination. He tells Giovanni that he will come to a
bad end. He wishes he had never met him. As to the coming
catastrophe, he suggests that on Giovanni's head be it, since his
(the Friar's) head will soon be beyond reach of it.

It is perhaps this unmistakable surrender by the Friar to the
impulse to run away and leave his protegés to their fate which
signals to us that there are clear limits to which this character's
words and values are to be trusted.[6] He is clearly an honest man.
Equally clearly, he is weak. This is not simply a matter of how
ineffectual he constantly seems to be against Giovanni's incestuous
will, but of his willingness to compromise moral standards for
people he favours. When he first persuades Annabella of her sin,
he immediately follows up his success with worldly counsel. She
must marry, to save her honour. Soranzo is waiting below – at
Florio's bidding, evidently – to hear her consent; which implies the
extent to which the Friar easily becomes Florio's tool. More, he

advises Annabella to marry, in the full knowledge that Annabella is already pregnant by Giovanni, and is already experiencing morning sickness. It seems here that the Friar is all too easily pushed into acting expediently, at the bidding of another, and in order to save his own face as spiritual advisor; yet at the same time the advice he gives seems neither ingeniously practical, nor highly-principled. He seems willing to sacrifice three people to the short-term appearance that the right things have been done.

In all, however well-meaning a figure Ford gives us in this Friar, the picture we finally get of him is one of timidity and defeat. Courage is clearly a major value in this play. It seems possessed neither by Soranzo, nor by his enemy Grimaldi, nor by the apparent major spokesman of the moral status quo.

Finally, there are the comparatively minor figures of Richardetto, Philotis and Bergetto. Richardetto is Hippolita's husband. Unbeknown to anyone but his niece, Philotis, Richardetto survived the journey to Leghorn, and now returns, in the disguise of a doctor, to the scene of his wife's frenzied affair with Soranzo, to avenge himself on her lover. Conveniently, Grimaldi arrives, presents himself as Soranzo's deadly rival for Annabella, and requests a suitably mortal poison for his enemy. Again, by the canons of revenge drama, Richardetto is something of a disappointment. Revenge by proxy is one stage less admirable still than Grimaldi's own furtiveness. When, later, Richardetto anticipates Grimaldi's success with a kind of brief parody of the bloodthirsty revenger's glee – 'So, if this hit, I'll laugh and hug revenge' (III.v.22) – our response might well be derisive. As to the niece whom he had rescued in Leghorn from orphanhood and potential predators, he now successfully urges her to marry Bergetto, the rich idiot whom she accidentally met and comforted with a codpiece point and a box of marmalade after one of his many humiliations. It is a match he hustles her into, as he later confesses, before Bergetto's guardian, Donado, has the chance to discover the business and object to it. Having bungled both his enterprises (the murder of Soranzo by Grimaldi, and the marriage of Philotis to Bergetto) by planning them both for the same night at the same place, so that Grimaldi mistakenly kills Bergetto, Richardetto bundles his niece into a nunnery, and lurks in disguise in the hope that someone else will come along to accomplish his revenge against Soranzo.

As to the likeable and amusing Bergetto himself, who comes to sexual maturity, at least, during the play, with his 'monstrous swelling about [his] stomach' when Philotis kisses him (III.v.45), he is a figure of considerable pity when murdered, and seems to have inspired affection in Philotis, in his keeper Poggio, even in his testy uncle, Donado. However, his function thematically in the play seems to be to define the word 'innocence' pejoratively. If innocence is idiocy, we are perhaps tempted to prefer experience, however extreme. More to the point, faced with two romantic couples in the play, the male of which is in both cases afflicted with some form of mental disorder, it would be hard not to prefer Annabella and Giovanni over Philotis and Bergetto. If the parallel were pushed further, and we saw both Giovanni and Bergetto die violent deaths – Bergetto passively and accidentally; Giovanni by his own active initiative, taking his enemies with him – the temptation is again to prefer Giovanni's way. Jacobean drama is full of death scenes which verge on the absurd, capped perhaps by those at the end of *Women Beware Women*, or perhaps the mock death of Flamineo in *The White Devil*. These absurd deaths, so much at odds with the earlier conventions of stage death as a serious and protracted summation of stage-life, seem to hint at an aura of absurdity permeating both human life and death. Bergetto's death falls within this category, however pathetically, as he feels his stab-wounds, and laments in words reminiscent of Flamineo's 'plumber in his guts' that his 'belly seethes like a porridge-pot' (III.vii.18) or that he is sure he 'cannot piss forward and backward, and yet [he is] wet before and behind' (11–12). There is perhaps a hint of the same kind of sense of the absurd in the earlier death of Hippolita, as she emerges somewhat incongruously from a masque of virgins, to drink, unknowingly, from the poisoned cup she had specifically prepared for Soranzo. Both deaths are heavily laden with irony. Again, if we care to compare them with the death-scenes of Giovanni and his sister, we cannot but be struck by the extent to which, taking things with extreme violence into his own hands, Giovanni must be granted to have governed his own final fate, and outpaced both human justice and immortal irony. In every respect, it seems that the minor figures are explicitly designed to fail in our eyes, and to leave us no alternative location for our concern but Giovanni and his sister. One by one the expected positives fail. The wronged Soranzo emerges as a bully and hypocrite, the Friar as a weakling, the rival suitor Grimaldi as a coward, and the wronged husband Richardetto as yet another. The kindly father Florio eventually tyrannizes, every scheme of revenge in the play is defeated, and innocence is represented by an idiot.[7] It is entertaining to think how unsavoury a portrait of normal life would remain in this play were we to remove the incest plot entirely. Had brother and sister never slept with each other, there would be little question of the despicable character of this at first apparently solid and sane bourgeois group. It would be a portrait worthy of Middleton's talent for scorn. It is against this background that Giovanni the moral explorer is set, and it would take no very extraordinary gifts for brother and sister to shine. After Ford gives Giovanni a perhaps deliberately misleading poor start, this is exactly what he and his sister do.

It is interesting to see what heroes Ford himself believes Giovanni to be linked with and similar to. In that respect, his borrowings are of particular use to us, since they tend to establish Giovanni's provenance. Perhaps surprisingly, all the most familiar fragments of quotation that Giovanni uses come neither from Caroline nor even Jacobean drama. They belong to a much older, heroic age, to the superman heroes of Elizabethan drama. It is probably no accident that these allusions, to the innocent titans of up to forty years previous to Ford's play, seem most prominent towards the end of the play, when Giovanni is most evidently outraging all normal values. They stake Giovanni's own claim, even as he commits himself to a course of extreme violation, to a kind of superhuman power, and to the extreme integrity of the superman heroes who never compromised with the world.

So, when taking his final leave of the Friar, Giovanni regards himself as a 'well-grown oak'; and, if he must fall, 'Some under-shrubs shall in my weighty fall/ Be crush'd to splits' (V.iii,end). The huge tree analogy ultimately goes back to Marlowe' *Tamburlaine*, but a nearer parallel is provided by Chapman's superman, Bussy D'Ambois.[8] Earlier in the same scene, Giovanni seems to recall Marlowe's hero Dr Faustus, when he tells the friar, 'The hell you oft have prompted is nought else/ But slavish and fond superstitious fear' (19–20). In his last scene with his sister, he still more distinctly recalls Tamburlaine's claim 'I hold the fates fast bound in iron chains,/ And with my hand turn Fortune's wheel about', in his line, 'why, I hold fate/ Clasp'd in my fist, and could command the course/ Of time's eternal motion' (V.v.11–13). His claim, 'revenge is mine' (V.vi.75) goes back as far as Kyd's Hieronimo in *The Spanish Tragedy*. It is by contrast Giovanni's enemies who evoke parallels with the more morally suspect characters of Jacobean drama. Thus, Vasques, wheedling information about the incestuous love-affair out of the nurse Putana, by pretended sympathy, and then brutally blinding her, reminds us strongly of Bosola's clever tricking of the Duchess of Malfi, and his later violent murder of the Duchess' maid Cariola. The outraged husband Soranzo, luring his wife and her lover into a trap, and even deliberately closeting them together before killing them, (only to be cheated of his revenge by their own initiative) reminds us point by point of Alsemero in Middleton's *The Changeling*, and his plan to murder Beatrice and DeFlores.

Nor are the superman heroes the only link favourable to Giovanni that Ford attempts to make. There is an unexpected echo of a John Donne love-poem ('Let sea-discoverers to new worlds have gone,/ let maps to others worlds on worlds have shown,/ Let us possess our world/ Each hath one and is one': *The Good-Morrow*) in his exclamation, 'Let poring book-men dream of other worlds,/ My world, and all of happiness, is here' (V.iii.13–14). Above all there is the sustained romantic parallel with Shakespeare's *Romeo and Juliet*.[9]

Ford, like Shakespeare, deals with two young lovers whose love is 'star-cross'd' and forbidden by accidents of family and birth. Both heroes have a worldly and well-meaning friar to help them. Both heroines are pushed towards an unwanted marriage by their fathers, but are aided towards gaining their true loves by a nurse. Both nurses are well-disposed to the desires of the flesh, but unable to understand any higher form of love than the 'ancient damnation' they favour. The heroine of *'Tis Pity She's a Whore* is even, like Juliet, given a balcony to sigh on. Whatever the differences between the two love-affairs, the strength of the parallels between the two plays do not seem to operate parodically, at the expense of Giovanni and Annabella. Rather, they would seem to establish that the later, incestuous pair are essentially analogous to the earlier innocents; that the same basic format of emotions is at stake, and that perhaps all that distinguishes them is what Giovanni repeatedly calls 'custom'.

Clearly, when Giovanni tells the sister he is about to kill, 'Pray, Annabella pray; since we must part,/ Go thou, white in thy soul, to fill a throne/ Of innocence and sanctity in Heaven' (V.v.63–5), or when Annabella describes her brother to her husband as 'So angel-like, so glorious, that a woman/ Who had not been but human, as I was,/ Would have kneel'd to him, and have begg'd for love' (IV.iii.37–9), they both believe in the 'heavenly' purity of their love, even if they find it difficult to believe in heaven. Before we surrender to the obvious temptation to moralize at this inconsistency, it is worth noticing that they alone in the play seem to live and die in that kind of confidence. When other characters mention religion it is almost invariably to predict or to call down the judgement of hell on each other, whether it be Florio complaining of the Cardinal shielding Grimaldi ('Heaven will judge them for't' – III.ix,end) or the assembled crowd watching the death of Hippolita ('Heaven, thou art righteous' – IV.i.89), or Richardetto predicting a bad end for his old enemy Soranzo ('there is One above/ Begins to work' – IV.ii.8–9). Yet in contrast to the death curses of Hippolita or Bergetto's pathetic conviction at his death that he is 'going the wrong way, sure' (III.vii.33), or Soranzo's fretful ranting at 'that black devil [Giovanni]' (V.vi.93), Giovanni himself dies confident that he will enjoy 'this *grace*./ Freely to view my Annabella's face' (107–8), and Annabella dies speaking of her brother, of forgiveness and of the mercy of 'great Heaven' (V.v.92–3). They and they alone seem capable of sustaining such thoughts, and this very striking fact is enough to complicate any thought of the mere blasphemy of their love-vocabulary. Rather, it might aptly seem to fit a pattern of life and death which is insistently associated with the fulfilment of some kind of higher destiny. Giovanni's early suggestion that "tis not . . ./ My lust, but 'tis my fate that leads me on' (I.ii.153–4) looks slightly less suspect, when Annabella reveals her own parallel compulsion towards him, long-felt but so deeply suppressed that she could 'scarcely think it' (247).

What the lovers evolve in their affair could justifiably be viewed as a code of morality which, however oddly distorted, has the capacity to convince us by its sheer power alone.[10] To themselves, they are moral heroes, and they conspicuously possess all the virtues which are lacking in the 'normal' world about them. In that world, fidelity is a scarce commodity, yet our lovers are virgins before their affair with each other, and remain intensely committed to each other, even despite Annabella's enforced marriage, which Giovanni sees as being likely 'to damn her! That's to prove/ Her greedy of variety of lust' (II.v.41–2). When, finally, he sees Soranzo's trap closing around them, he kills his sister to save her fame, to avenge himself on Soranzo and to uphold the value of honour:

> To save thy fame, and kill thee in a kiss.
> Thus die, and die by me, and by my hand!
> Revenge is mine; honor doth love command
>
> (V.v.84–6)

If fidelity is something the lovers seem able to boast, so too is honesty in a dissimulating world. Both are innocent of the sort of bed-tricks and devices which are the stock-in-trade of such as Beatrice and DeFlores in *The Changeling*. Instead, Annabell seems almost to flaunt her pregnancy, once married, while Giovanni is so unable to dissemble that he risks a very early detection by his refusal to toast his sister's marriage. Later, he tells Vasques baldly that he 'dares' to go to Soranzo's treacherous feast, and it is indeed this third quality, of courage, which it is above all the lovers' glory to possess. They go not blindly but knowingly into the traps of their enemies and into unheard-of paths of violence, alike. Conspicuous is Annabella's behaviour under her husband's brutal jealousy. As he threatens her, she defies him as a 'beastly man' compared with 'the man,/ The more than man, that got this sprightly boy' (IV.iii.15, 30–1). As he then swings and drags her about by the hair, she quite remarkably begins to sing in Italian, a song of how sweet it is to die for love (59); all along refusing to reveal, even under the direst threats, the identity of her lover. Singing again of dying with god's grace, she seems almost at this stage to have reached a state of spiritual ecstasy comparable with that of sainthood. The more she suffers, the more completely she seems to reach a condition of spiritual fulfillment.

Giovanni's is merely a more extreme version still of the same condition. Digging in his sister's corpse for her heart, he seems to attain some kind of almost contemplative stillness, spinning gruesome conceits of how his heart is entombed within it, and how her womb was both the cradle and the grave of the foetus they had made. Most memorable, though, is his statement, as he stands with her heart on his dagger that 'in my fists I bear the twists of life' (V.vi.72). Common sense would rather suggest that what he held were the proofs of death, yet these veins and arteries seem at this moment to make him live with an energy far more intense than those around him. He is scarcely brought down, even by the Banditti. He seems little short of inspired.[11] However absurd it seems for Giovanni to translate his appalled father's heart attack in this scene as a becoming act of courage (65–7), Giovanni's whole thrust in these last scenes is towards such transformations.

From the start, Giovanni seemed to his friend the friar as a 'man remark'd', set apart from others. He has extraordinary capacities for self-dedication, yet the ends he devotes them to are almost inevitably abnormal. Indeed, they are a more or less deliberate quest into the forbidden; as the Friar says, 'Thou hast left the schools/ Of knowledge to converse with lust and death' (I.i.57–8).[12] Both 'conversations' seem actually brief. Annabella's marriage and repentance almost immediately separate their lust. They hardly appear together from the beginning of Act Two up to their final, fatal interview in Act V. Giovanni himself has only 125 lines in the interim, divided between two scenes with the Friar and one with Putana. By Act Five all that is left is death.[13] Yet while this career too is brief, it is a course which he knows will win him a 'glorious death', an 'act [he] glor[ies] in', his 'last and greater part' (V.iii.76, V.v.91, 106). In two blindingly theatrical scenes, he accomplishes what he has to, immune to the tirades of the righteous. When he dies, all that is left is Vasques, boasting of how he blinded an old woman, and the Cardinal, sweeping up the financial leavings. For Giovanni, death is 'a long look'd for guest' (105), and a release from what drove him on. Yet, however briefly, he had been Ford's inspired explorer in a morally muddy 'normal' world, and no single other Jacobean moral experimenter can boast anything like the appalling discoveries he had made.[14]

7
Shakespeare

Shakespeare's profound allegiance to received moral ideas is rarely contested and will not be, here. Not until the end of his career as an author did he write for anything other than the popular theatre, and even when the Blackfriars was available, his plays seem also to have been played at the Globe. Like most of the dramatists in the popular tradition, he was a moral conservative, and it would therefore be most unlikely that he should be attracted to the drama of moral experiment. He tried it only once, in *Measure for Measure*, just as he tried his hand at satiric drama once, in *Troilus and Cressida*. In the case of *Measure for Measure*, the attempt came right at the beginning of the new King's reign, and is one of the very earliest dramas of experiment. He was actually helping to define and promote the form, even if *Measure for Measure* is by no means wholly committed to the impulse to experiment morally. Aside from this single play, though, the drama of moral experiment is conspicuously absent from his work.

Indeed, his lack of permanent attraction to it may be stated more strongly than this. It is not simply that Shakespeare dabbled once and then left the new form strictly alone. Actually, the plays he went on to write may bear a negative relationship with the drama of moral experiment: that is, they may be written actively to contest the idea of experimentation, and to reassert the values which lie most opposite to moral enquiry. In particular, they assert the value of faith: not so much religious faith, as faith in the close ties of kinship and marriage. These are the very areas which the more radical dramatists of the time choose as most promising for moral experiment, most likely to yield vivid results. What Shakespeare may ultimately owe to the drama of moral experiment may therefore be the whole motive force behind his greatest tragedies and his late comedies. If *Othello* or *King Lear* or *The Tempest* contain strong themes of the importance of faith, and the survival of filial or matrimonial loyalty, we may owe these themes to Shakespeare's intense moral reaction against the moral tamperings of his contemporaries.

To begin with the play he wrote in the same year as *Measure for Measure* – *Othello* – it is notable that it revolves, like *Measure for Measure*, and like so much else of the drama of moral experiment, around the idea of doubting a woman's chastity. Like the experimenters, Othello constantly demands proof either way of his wife's purity. Like them also, he seems to discover, through a kind of test, that she is false. The only difference of course is that actually his wife is pure, and the 'test' is a simple trick, played on him by his pretended friend and ally, Iago.[1]

The incident concerned is the only one where Othello is given something solid to go on, regarding his wife's 'infidelity'. For the rest, all that fuels his jealousy is his own insecurity and Iago's hints and anecdotes. Here, at least, he is able apparently to see and hear Cassio boasting to Iago of his conquest of Desdemona. Thanks to an unhappy coincidence, he also sees Cassio's mistress Bianca return to her lover the very handkerchief which was Othello's own first love-gift to Desdemona, and which – as Iago told him in an earlier scene – Desdemona had now given to Cassio. The scene is of course a simple fraud. Iago had stationed Othello just close enough to see distinctly but not close enough to hear every word. The words he misses are when Iago prompts Cassio to talk of Bianca. What he then hears is Cassio's dismissive jokes about Bianca's infatuation with him. Unfortunately, with suspicion already planted in his mind, he then construes all these jokes to apply to Desdemona. The handkerchief is a fortuitous final confirmation. After this point, he strikes his wife in public, openly calls her strumpet, and in their next scene together murders her.

The scene is therefore a critical one in giving Othello the final push towards violence. Interestingly, Iago is prompted to stage it by Othello's own demand for what he calls 'ocular proof':

> Villain, be sure thou prove my love a whore,
> Be sure of it, give me the ocular proof,
> Or by the worth of man's eternal soul,
> Thou hadst been better have been born a dog,
> Than answer my wak'd wrath . . .
> Make me to see't, or at the least so prove it,
> That the probation bear no hinge, nor loop,
> To hang a doubt on; or woe upon thy life!

(III.iii.365–72)

Later he confesses, 'I think my wife be honest, and I think she is not,/ I think thou art just, and think thou art not' (390–1). He wishes above all to be sure either way ('Would I were satisfied'), and again demands 'I'll have some proof' (392), and 'Give me a living reason she's disloyal' (415). What Iago agrees to provide is circumstantial evidence – 'Imputation and strong circumstances,/ Which lead directly to the door of truth' (412–3) – and proceeds to tell the story of overhearing Cassio's sexual dream about Desdemona, and having seen Cassio wipe his beard with Desdemona's handkerchief. These he presents as corroborating evidence: 'this may help to thicken other proofs' (436); and, 'It speaks against her, with the other proofs' (448). The entire section hinges on Othello's need to be out of uncertainty. It is as if he would prefer to hear the worst than merely to doubt. To meet this need, Iago has only to invent the most threadbare lies. Othello's belief in them is immediate and ferocious: 'I'll tear her all to pieces' (438).

It is, then, exactly this demand for proof which is Othello's undoing. Where he might have been expected to have faith in his wife, he prefers instead to believe the evidence of his own eyes. Unfortunately, he is already predisposed to doubt his wife's fidelity, so that whatever he sees he is likely to interpret against her. Once he has seen Cassio joking with Iago, his doubts become absolute. From this point onward, no honest denial by her has any power to penetrate his conviction that she is unfaithful.

Clearly, then, Shakespeare is already forming his own response to the very drama of moral experiment to which he himself gave some impetus in the same year. *Othello* seems written actively to contest the idea of experiment, or proof, or trial, and to show its destructive effect on an honest man. Othello's doubts and insecurities as a black, and an outsider, generate his ironic flight from faith into credulity, and his belief only in 'proof'. Unable to believe in himself, he cannot believe in Desdemona's love for him.

The same basic pattern had been rehearsed in *Much Ado About Nothing*. There, Claudio was deluded into believing that he had seen his wife-to-be, Hero, courting a man at her window on the very eve of the wedding. Claudio, who has already demonstrated his own insecurity earlier in the play, immediately translates what he sees into proof of Hero's treachery, and, at the wedding, repudiates her and 'kills' her. There is one other character – Beatrice – who has absolute faith in her cousin's innocence, and two others – Benedick and the Friar – who carefully 'note' Hero, and try to sift the evidence to find the truth. Claudio, however, submits to the lure of proof, and to Don John's challenge, 'If you dare not trust that you see, confess not that you know'. He therefore misplaces his trust, and comes close to destroying innocence. *Othello* simply sharpens this pattern. The indignation of the worldly-wise Emilia is our guide to the right response to any suggestion that Desdemona is untrue. Othello has far more cause for trust than Claudio, but demands 'ocular proof' instead. In doing so, he not only destroys an innocent wife, but also contaminates and destroys his own innocence.

Othello is therefore a kind of negative lesson, aimed against experimentation. *King Lear* advances the argument one more stage, by promoting and reinforcing the very doctrine of human ties and bonds that the experimental heroes of Jacobean drama deliberately set out to violate. If Mendoza in *The Malcontent* boasts, in dedicating himself to evil, that 'Nothing so holy,/ No band of nature so strong,/ No law of friendship so sacred,/ But I'll profane, burst, violate' (II.i.13–16), he is after all tacitly acknowledging that human ties have a kind of sacredness. The idea is at least as old as Boethius' theory of a divine love inspiring the universe, and generating the natural laws which unite and restrain the elements, so that the sea and land, earth and sky 'loven hem togidres . . . bounde by love'. In the same way, Boethius argues, love 'halt togidres peples joyned with an holy boond, and knetteth sacrement of chaste loves'.[2] Shakespeare's earlier plays treat the human bond in terms of an affinity, by blood or by choice. In *Julius Caesar*, the conspirators protest that they need no spur to endeavour, no vow to secrecy, beyond their shared Roman-ness: 'What other bond/ Than secret Romans, that have spoke the word/ And will not palter'. Later, Portia appeals to the 'bond of marriage . . . that great vow/ That did incorporate and make us one', to urge that Brutus should confide his plans to her. In both cases, the speakers regard themselves as being of one flesh together, and therefore by right sharing every value, every assumption with each other. It is this, similarly, that Le Beau means in *As You Like It*, when he describes how Rosalind's and Celia's love for each other is 'dearer than the natural bond of sisters'; a love they finally only surrender to the still more binding tie of marriage, 'great Juno's crown . . . (the) blessed bond of board and bed'.

What King Lear does is to define the idea of a bond more carefully, and far more forcefully. This act of redefinition includes some rec-

ognition that a human bond has an almost legally binding force.
When Cordelia refuses to compete with her sisters in protestations
of love for Lear, she does so in quasi-legal terms:

> Unhappy that I am, I cannot heave
> My heart into my mouth; I love your majesty
> According to my bond; nor more nor less.

(I.i.91–3)

It seems that Cordelia is recognizing that the gift of life from the
parent brings with it obligations in the child, but that those obligations are circumscribed and limited. Though the most truly loving
of the daughters, Cordelia sees clear contractual limits to the extent
to which she must repay a debt. True, she currently 'return[s] those
duties back as are right fit'. Yet, when she marries, 'That lord whose
hand must take [her] plight shall carry/ Half [her] love with him,
half [her] cares and duty' (97, 101–2).

Right from the earliest plays the purely natural sense of a bond
as affinity had existed alongside some sense of contractual arrange-
ment. It centres around the idea of life itself being granted by god
or Nature; a grant with strings attached. So, in *Richard III*, Queen
Margaret prays god to 'cancel his bond of life' (Richard's); and in
Henry IV part I, Hal pleads that his father give him the chance, at
the battle of Shrewsbury, to wipe away the record of his prodigality
in Eastcheap – 'If not, the end of life cancels all bands'. The lease
on life here seems to come with a clear set of moral obligations as
payment. The payments lapse with the leesee's death. It seems as
if the idea of a 'lease of life' lies behind these phrases. The phrase
does not actually occur until Dryden, but Shakespeare certainly
seems to have connected the idea of life to the idea of a lease. So,
in sonnet 146, he forbids his soul to pay much attention to his
body's appearance: 'Why so large cost, having so short a lease?'
Macbeth hopes, whatever the witches prophesy, to die a natural
death: to 'live the lease of nature, pay his breath/ To time and mortal
custom'.

Interestingly, he here thinks of paying his debt to nature only in
terms of a breath. Other Shakespearean characters recognise that
the payments are higher. Coriolanus, for instance, having defected
to the Volsci, and intending to renounce his wife, mother and child,
shouts 'out, affection!/ All bond and privilege of nature break'. It

would be consistent with some interpretations of Coriolanus' last phase that he here denies nature's claims in their mutual bond, knowing that nature would swiftly retaliate, and revoke his lease of life. Even Macbeth is aware that, simply by living, he is partner in some kind of bargain, and fights against it. Believing that he must kill Banquo to make his throne safe, he makes his prayer to the powers of darkness: 'Come seeling night,/ Scarf up the tender eye of pitiful day;/ And with thy bloody and invisible hand/ Cancel and tear to pieces that great bond/ Which keeps me pale'. It is the clearest of references to a document between nature and the individual human life; whose terms dictate a humane and moral life to the leesee. Earlier, Macbeth had challenged his wife's coarse definition of manhood: 'I dare do all that may become a man./ Who dares do more is none'. Now, he fights against a moral definition of manhood, the moral restraints which keep him pale, and strains to cancel the agreement which binds him to them.

In *King Lear*, this legalistic meaning of the word is interestingly reinforced by the idea of the obligations of love being part of an entire fabric by which all natural things are restrained and governed. As in Boethius, there is a close relationship between human love, and God's larger unifying love. So, when Gloucester is deceived into thinking that Edgar is plotting his death, it is in terms of universal chaos that he interprets his son's 'treachery':

> These late eclipses in the sun and moon
> portend no good to us: though the wisdom of
> nature should reason it thus and thus, yet Nature
> finds itself scourg'd by the sequent effects. Love
> cools, friendship falls off, brothers divide: in
> cities, mutinies; in countries, discord; in
> palaces, treason; and the bond cracked 'twixt
> son and father. . . . We have seen
> the best of our time: machinations, hollowness,
> treachery, and all ruinous disorders follow
> us unquietly to our graves.
>
> (I.ii.107–20)

Though the bastard Edmund despises his father's superstition, the play as a whole seems to support Gloucester's thesis, with nature in commotion in the gigantic storm, as it responds to so many disturbances in the natural order of human affairs. It is as if the play witnesses or enacts sins so primal as to produce a fissure in the entire fabric of things. 'The offices of nature, bond of childhood/ Effects of courtesy, dues of gratitude' are stressed equally by the wronged king, stripped of his retinue; or by Edmund, pretending to have urged Edgar not to take their father's life, and pleading 'with how manifold and strong a bond/ The child was bound to the father'. The theory of bonds that should be inviolable is well known by both victim and wrongdoer. When the wrongs are done, there is an intriguing shift in the language of the play from bonds to contracts. Regan's husband Albany ironically forbids his widowed sister-in-law, Goneril to marry Edmund, since Edmund is already promised:

> for your claim, fair sister,
> I bar it in the interest of my wife;
> 'Tis she is sub-contracted to this lord
> And I, her husband, contradict your banes.

> (V.iii.85–8)

There is also an interesting shift to reverse all values. The knave Oswald, speaking of the disgust Albany begins to feel for his wife's doings, seems outraged:

> I told him of the army that was landed;
> He smiled at it: I told him you were coming;
> His answer was "The worse": of Gloucester's treachery,
> And of the loyal service of his son,
> When I inform'd him, then he called me sot,
> And told me I had turned the wrong side out:
> Which most he should dislike seems pleasant to him;
> What like, offensive.

> (IV.ii.4–11)

The thought is immediately confirmed by Goneril's description of her husband as a 'milk-liver'd man', when he speaks of her offences and the way they threaten such a return to primal barbarity that 'Humanity must perforce prey on itself,/ Like monsters of the deep'. Only in the saving loyalty of Edgar and Cordelia is there any surviving hope. As a Gentleman says, Cordelia is the single daughter

'Who redeems nature from the general curse/ Which twain have brought her to' (IV.vi.207–8). Both negatively, therefore, and positively, the play makes the strongest case for the concept of 'nature' as a uniting, disciplining force, tying men and women together in 'bonds' both of obligation, and restraint. There is the strongest accompanying implication that, once those bonds are tampered with, it creates a 'breach in . . . abused nature'. Interestingly, what caused the rupture was Lear's decision to ask for proof.[3] He cannot trust love, and must hear instead protestations of it. By contrast, Cordelia's husband, France, when he hears of her disgrace, will not believe that she has committed any offence 'of such unnatural degree' as to merit such a punishment:

> which to believe of her
> Must be a faith that reason without miracle
> Might never plant in me.

(I.i.221–3)

This striking testimony of faith is yet another confirmation of the strength of the play's deliberate counter-statement against the scepticism and destructiveness of experiments.[4]

If *King Lear* merely seeks trivial and unnecessary proofs, Macbeth is a character far more radically inquisitive. From the first encounter with the witches, in which, having established that they are 'aught/ That man may question' (I.iii.42), he insistently quizzes them, and demands to know the very source of their 'strange Intelligence' (76), it is Macbeth, not Banquo, who pushes his enquiry to its limits.[5] Banquo's response is to greet the news with caution. The witches may be from the devil. Their quest might be to damn, through alluring promises. The reality of that possibility is promptly shown in Macbeth's next soliloquy. Despite his insistence that the Witches are morally neutral – 'This supernatural soliciting/ Cannot be ill; cannot be good' (130–1) – he so immediately produces the idea not only of becoming king, but of achieving the throne through 'murder' (139) as to confirm Banquo's suspicion of a devilish temptation. Already, his mind is full of speculation and what he calls 'surmise' (141). In short, Macbeth is not the kind of man who could ever accede to his own suggestion that, 'If Chance will have me King, why Chance may crown me/ Without my stir' (144–5). He cannot submit to his own fate. He must more actively 'take a bond

of Fate' (IV.i.84). The legalistic terminology is an indication of the
way Macbeth abandons his human allegiances. Still believing that
he can 'live the lease of Nature, pay his breath/ To time, and mortal
custom' (99–100), he reveals the frailty of his remaining tie with
nature in the same scene. Meeting the witches once more, he
demands knowledge at any cost:

> Though you untie the winds, and let them fight
> Against the Churches; though the yesty waves
> Confound and swallow navigation up;
> Though bladed corn be lodg'd, and trees blown down;
> Though castles topple on their warders' heads;
> Though palaces, and pyramids, do slope
> Their heads to their foundations; though the treasure
> Of Nature's germens tumble all together,
> Even till destruction sicken, answer me
> To what I ask you.

(52–61)

By this stage, he is 'bent to know,/ By the worst means, the worst'
(III.iv.133–4). There is little to gratify the quest, other than the search
itself. Paradoxically, the drive for knowledge reduces him from
being a speculative man to being an automaton. As early as the
end of Act One scene four, Macbeth is speaking of allowing the
eye to wink at the hand (52). Later, he determines increasingly to
cancel any interim of thought between conceiving and enacting:
'Strange things I have in head, that will to hand,/ Which must be
acted, ere they may be scann'd' (III.iv.138–9); or later, and more
famously, 'The very firstlings of my heart shall be/ The firstlings of
my hand' (IV.i.147–8). It is this unnatural progeny with which he
is left, when he abandons natural things, to embark on his long
and irreversible voyage of enquiry. By contrast, Banquo stifles his
enquiry, and retains his humanity. Clearly tempted by the idea that
'by the verities on [Macbeth] made good,/ May they not be my
oracles as well,/ And set me up in hope?' (III.i.8–10), he immediately
suppresses the thought: 'But, hush; no more' (10). Macbeth later
speaks enviously of Banquo's 'royalty of nature' (III.i.49), and specifically identifies this with his notable moral caution, 'that doth
guide his valour/ To act in safety' (52–3). That moral caution brings
Banquo peace of mind. By contrast, of course, Macbeth's mental

restlessness plunges him finally into mental torment, a 'torture of the mind' (III.ii.21). His curiosity translates into distrust, even of the murderers he sends against Banquo. He taints all those around him to the extent that Malcolm cannot trust his allies. Finally, Macbeth's need to manufacture his fate and his future becomes the arid disavowal of that future as the emptiest succession of 'tomorrows'.

If the great tragedies seem designed to demonstrate the catastrophes which befall the protagonists and their worlds once the experimental urge is unleashed, the last comedies appear both to share that design, and to provide, with their renewed stress on faith, something of an alternative.[6] These plays continue to include some clearly identifiable 'experimental' components, such as the chastity test, or the disguise of nobility, but they are deployed so as to disgrace the idea of experiment, or in ways wholly antithetical to the idea of experiment. It is innocence which emerges as the true subject of these plays, and the miraculous capacity of innocence to survive evil is what we are invited to pin our faith on, and rejoice in.

Cymbeline is of course the stuff of fairy-tale, with imperilled heroine, villain and hero, and wicked stepmother; it is set within the scope of a recognizable civilized culture, ancient Rome, whose authority and right to tribute are recognized at the end of the play. However, the setting is also to some extent barbaric, the furthest corners of an ancient Britain which is the furthest Western outpost of that empire, and it is also clearly pagan, not Christian. This choice serves to stress the possibility of a strong force of 'natural' goodness in man, and its stubborn refusal to compromise, however beset. However, almost immediately, that goodness is put to exactly the sort of test familiar in the drama of moral experiment. The hero Posthumus, virtuous but banished husband of the heroine Imogen, is foolishly provoked into a wager with the young Roman seducer, Iachimo, regarding Imogen's purity and fidelity. He agrees as a result of the wager to submit his wife to temptation, confident of her ability to pass the test.[7]

Unfortunately, the two men have a very different conception of their bet. For Posthumus, the trial will be an honest one. For Iachimo, it becomes a challenge to win at all costs. Since he uses deception to achieve his end, he represents the typical experimenter of Jacobean drama. Indeed, from his very first words in the play it is evident that he shares the unfocused disaffection that so strongly characterizes the type. In his test of Imogen, he feigns shock, lies heartily about Posthumus' infidelity to Imogen, and offers her the chance of 'revenge'. The former part of this seems to win some belief from Imogen, since she responds, 'My lord, I fear,/ Has forgot Britain'. However, her very next impulse is to try to suppress what she is hearing: 'Let me hear no more'; and as soon as Iachimo begins to reveal his own designs on her, her response is an immediate and ferocious repulse. His attempt to exploit for his own purposes the anger he has hoped to provoke is her proof that his whole endeavour is impure:

> Away, I do condemn mine ears, that have
> So long attended thee. If thou wert honourable
> Thou wouldst have told this tale for virtue, not
> For such an end thou seek'st, as base as strange.
> Thou wrong'st a gentleman who is as far
> From thy report as thou from honour, and
> Solicits here a lady that disdains
> Thee and the devil alike.

(I.vii.141–8)

It is at this stage, when simple deception has failed, that Iachimo's methods become more fully duplicitous. The experiment has failed, but the experimenter is undeterred: he will simply fake the results. His first moves in this direction take the form of an interesting distinction. The test, he claims, was not a test, but a trial. In an image unique to this play, he pretends to Imogen that he only said such things to make sure that she was as good as her reputation, and worthy of Posthumus' love: 'the love I bear him/ Made me fan you thus' (175–6). The image is of the winnowing of corn, the separation of the grain from the chaff. Iachimo merely wanted to expose the true and wholesome inner character of Imogen, by blowing away the chaff of exterior politeness. Like many earlier figures, the figures primarily of romance, he wished in other words to prove that Imogen was true; unlike the protagonists of experimental drama, who fundamentally wish to demonstrate that apparent virtue is actually false.

The trick works, and Imogen accepts him as a virtuous tester. He exploits her restored trust, by concealing himself in a trunk which he pretends contains valuables which need to be kept in a safe place – such as her bedchamber. In the night, as she sleeps, he steals from the trunk, takes careful notes of the appearance of the bedchamber and of the sleeping woman (the mole on her breast and so forth), and, stealing her bracelet, creeps back into the trunk undetected. Subsequently, he makes his way back to Rome and boasts his conquest to Posthumus, who, on the evidence of the descriptions and the bracelet, believes him. In this way, the experiment's results are falsified.

At this point, Shakespeare's drift becomes evident. It is clear that, apart of course from Iachimo, the character we are most clearly asked to condemn is Posthumus. Iachimo is merely the carefully created serpent, whose scheme achieves the fall, not of a woman, but of a man. It is Posthumus' lack of faith in his wife which is the issue.[8] Like Othello, he trusts 'proof'. Just as Othello is tricked, so too Posthumus finds himelf deceived by 'simular proof' (V.v.200). Like Othello, too, Posthumus seems rapidly to rush towards the worst conviction, as soon as his first resistance is down. Iachimo's description of Imogen's bedchamber he is able to brush aside. However, the production of her bracelet instantly overcomes his trust:

> Here, take this, too; [*Gives the ring*]
> It is a basilisk unto mine eye,
> Kills me to look on't. Let there be no honour
> Where there is beauty: truth where semblance: love
> Where there's another man. The vows of women
> Of no more bondage be to where they are made
> Than they are to their virtues, which is nothing.
> O, above measure false!

(II.iv.106–13)

It is a bystander who points out that this tirade is premature, and that the bracelet could have been stolen. Posthumus eagerly seizes this comfort, and retrieves the ring, only to abandon it just as abruptly, on Iachimo's bald denial:

> Hark you, he swears: by Jupiter he swears.
> 'Tis true, nay, keep the ring, 'tis true: I am sure
> She would not lose it. . . . . No, he hath enjoyed her.

(123–6)

He now positively thrusts the ring back at Iachimo, and refuses to listen to those who urge that 'This is not strong enough to be believ'd/ Of one persuaded well of' (131–2). The phrase, 'persuaded well of', means 'well thought of'. In other words, no-one of Imogen's high reputation should be lightly convicted. However, this wise counsel is lost on Posthumus. Iachimo has achieved his purpose, without even exhausting the stock of his 'evidence'. Only now does he refer to the mole beneath Imogen's breast, provoking another particularly Othello-like outburst: 'O that I had her here, to tear her limb-meal!/ I will go there and do't i'th'court, before/ Her father. I'll do something [Exit]'.

As with *Othello*, there is a fiercely loyal independent witness to the innocent lady's loyalty: here, Pisanio, who responds to Posthumus' demand that he should murder Imogen with a horror that duly puts his master's doubts in perspective:

> How, of adultery? Wherefore write you not
> What monster's her accuser? Leonatus!
> O master, what a strange infection
> Is fall'n into thy ear! What false Italian,
> (As poisonous tongu'd as handed) hath prevail'd
> On thy too ready hearing? Disloyal? No.
> She's punish'd for her truth, and undergoes,
> More goddess-like than wife-like, such assaults
> As would take in some virtue. O my master,
> Thy mind to her is now as low as were
> Thy fortunes.

(III.ii.1–11)

Of course, Imogen's own frantic eagerness, in the same scene, to seize any chance to join her husband, at whatever risk, fully and poignantly makes the same point.

The issues of faith as against 'proof' continue to echo through the play. On its first appearance in the play, the minor action featuring Cymbeline's two lost sons, Guidarius and Arviragus, and their supposed father Belarius, introduces the same issue. Belarius tells the boys his oft-told tale of how he, a faithful warrior, was nevertheless cast off by Cymbeline, when 'two villains, whose false oaths prevailed/ Before my perfect honour, swore to Cymbeline/ I was confederate with the Romans' (III.iii.66–8). Then comes the scene (III.iv) where Imogen, taken to Wales by Pisanio, is shown Posthumus' letter, speaking of 'proof as strong as [his] grief' of her adultery. Her indignation takes the interesting form of the conclusion that Posthumus has been untrue to her. One undermining of faith clearly produces another, and Imogen now seeks a martyrdom on Pisanio's sword which will prove to Posthumus – when he tires of what she is convinced has perverted him (an Italian mistress) – what a 'strain of rareness' he lost in her. It is with some difficulty that Pisanio manages to replace this idea with the alternative, that Posthumus has been betrayed, not by a woman, but by a man.

The subordinate plot develops, of Imogen's disguise as a boy, her ignorant meeting with her lost brothers, of Cloten's jealous pursuit of her in Posthumus' clothing, of Guiderius' slaughter of him in fair fight, of Imogen's 'death' and revival, and her discovery of Cloten's body. In each item of it, the paramount issue seems to be of evidence as against instinct and faith. The comic-plot commonplaces of disguise – here present in a double measure – or of apparent death, or of high birth obscured in humble surroundings seem here especially directed towards a theme of the deceptiveness of appearances. Individually, they had all appeared in romance generally, and in Shakespeare's earlier comedies. Here, they seem present in unusual density, and the intended theme seems especially clear in the light of the comparative accuracy of instinctive judgement. Instinctive knowledge is evident from our first acquaintance with Guiderius and Arviragus, who, Belarius tells us, 'know little they are sons to the king . . . and though trained up thus meanly,/ I'th'cave wherein they bow, their thoughts do hit/ The roofs of palaces, and nature prompts them/ In simple and low things to prince it much/ Beyond the trick of others' (III.iii.80–6). Instinct, then, strongly impels them to good.[9] It continues to do so, in for instance their recognition of a natural affinity for Imogen. Their initial shock at finding her in their cave, and their reaction to her offer of money for their food, so quickly subside that, within only twenty lines of meeting her, they are captivated by her. The instinctive recognition is mutual. Just as quickly, Imogen is already speaking of 'brothers', and claiming that she'd 'change [her] sex to be companion with them' (III.vii.60). In their next scene together, both brothers confess that they love her at least as much as they love their 'father'. Arviragus goes so far as to say, 'The bier at the door,/ And a demand who is't shall die, I'ld say/ "My father, not this youth"' (IV.ii.22–4). Belarius responds not with any sense of hurt feelings, but with a renewed apostrophe to their 'worthiness of nature, breed of greatness'. He returns to this theme, almost insistently, when summing up in soliloquy the events surrounding the killing of Cloten. Himself a war hero, he had dreaded the outcome. They, however, had been defiant of the consequences, and Belarius wonders at their untaught and wonderful combination of tenderest courtesy and dauntless courage: "Tis wonder/ That an invisible instinct should frame them/ To royalty unlearned, honour untaught,/ Civility not seen from other, valour/ That wildly grows in them, but yields a crop/ As if it had been sow'd' (IV.ii.176–81). All this adds to the idea of benign knowledge, instinctively held.

When Imogen awakes from her death-like sleep, and finds herself lying next to the headless body of Cloten dressed in Posthumus' clothes, she of course believes that Posthumus is dead: 'this is his hand:/ His foot Mercurial: his Martial thigh:/ The brawns of Hercules' (IV.ii.309–11). Poignantly, she falls on the body of the man she hated, crying, 'O, my lord, my lord' (332). It is hard to blame Imogen for this, or even for her immediate conclusion that Pisanio conspired with Cloten to murder her husband. All one can say is that this is the most conclusive tragi-comic proof of the inadequacy of visible 'evidence'. What she sees as 'pregnant' and 'confirm[ed]' is no more than a trick of disguise. The Duke of *Measure for Measure* had deliberately juggled with the identity of amputated heads, on the supposition that 'death's a great disguiser'; the substitutions greatly helped in his experiment on the virtues and vices of his subjects. Here, identical decapitated bodies are used in a quite contrary cause: to show that even Faith (Imogen's assumed name is Fidele) can be tricked by apparent proofs. Nevertheless, Faith is still the superior quality. At the end of the scene, Pisanio, alone at court, under suspicion for the disappearances of Imogen and Cloten, and ignorant of all that has happened, refers himself to time, fortune and the heavens for a solution. Similarly, Posthumus, now back in Britain, with the 'evidence' of Imogen's bloodied clothes to suggest that Pisanio has indeed killed her as instructed, now commits himself fully to the gods' will; fighting on Britain's side against the Romans. Again, part of the interest of the scene is the idea of native and instinctive worth. He appeals to the blood of his forebears, the lion-hearted Leonati, to shine through his disguise, as indeed it does. Yet his abandonment to the gods' will works in unanticipated ways, since their will is to reward, not to punish. His parents' ghosts, praying to the gods to spare their son more suffering, are answered by Jupiter, the literal *deus ex machina*, with the news that Posthumus's misfortunes were a kind of appetizer: 'Whom best I love I cross; to make my gift/ The more delayed,

delighted' (V.iv.101–2). So, in the end, prayers are answered, and
he who surrenders himself to the will of the gods is rewarded.

The final act duly disentangles all the confused narrative knots,
with the king confessing his confusion concerning what he thought
he knew about the queen who is now disclosed to have been so
wicked:

> Mine eyes
> Were not in fault, for she was beautiful;
> Mine ears that heard her flattery, nor my heart
> That thought her like her seeming. It had been vicious
> To have mistrusted her: yet, O my daughter,
> That it was folly in me thou mayst say,
> And prove it in thy feeling.

(V.v.62–8)

Altogether, the message of 'faith' is not an uncomplicated one.
Clearly, we are taught that, to doubt a woman of well-known virtue
on slender evidence is close to sinning; but even the most trusting
are capable of being deceived by similar visual evidence; and the
case of Cymbeline and his wife shows that it is possible to mis-place
faith, and trust it too far. The last comic twist of the theme is when
Posthumus, crying 'O Imogen!/ My queen, my life, my wife! O
Imogen,/ Imogen, Imogen', is intercepted by Imogen in disguise,
who steps forward to reveal all, and is promptly struck by him for
daring to interrupt his grief. One might add that it is, ironically,
physical evidence – of Arviragus' swaddling mantle, and Guiderius'
mole – that convinces Cymbeline that the two strangers are indeed
his sons. The play ends, however, with prayers to the gods, and
an oracle fulfilled. Without doubt, the major thematic direction is
away from empirical proof, towards faith in the enduring qualities
of natural virtues and affinities, and also towards some kind of
human balance between credulity and doubt. Above all, perhaps,
it is a play which sets out to demonstrate the evil of moral experiment, by taking one of the major devices of the experiment-play,
the chastity test, and showing its corrosive consequences on people
who remain essentially good, but shaken in their faith. As ever,
with Shakespeare's late plays, evil is fairly readily identifiable, at
least by an audience, and is clearly outnumbered by good. Its powers to convert the good to its cause are here as severely limited as
in that most famous of Shakespeare's plays using a pagan setting,

King Lear. Yet, the vulnerable point of good is clearly its faith, or the potential failure of it, and *Cymbeline* seems designed here as a cautionary tale. Its highly elaborate denouement, and especially Shakespeare's preparedness to risk the device of the *deus ex machina* seem also to point towards a strong devotional element in the play, with the happy ending serving as a somewhat more than routine, more than merely conventionally comic, statement of faith in the survival of good.

Shakespeare reverts to the idea of female fidelity, set against irrational male jealousy, in *The Winter's Tale*. Criticism of the play has always argued that we need not take Leontes' sudden distrust of his wife as a realistic depiction, but rather accept it as a dramatic 'given'. Yet, its suddenness may indeed be a deliberate point rather than a piece of dramatic expediency.[10] The unreasonableness may serve as a deliberate exaggeration of an issue. Again, the issue is of faith. Leontes, as everyone points out, sometimes at considerable personal risk, has no reason to suspect his wife. What he believes, though, is that his observation of her gives him clearest visible evidence of her infidelity:

> Is whispering nothing?
> Is leaning cheek to cheek? Is meeting noses?
> Kissing with inside lip? stopping the career
> Of laughter with a sigh (a note infallible
> Of breaking honesty)? horsing foot on foot?
> Skulking in corners? wishing clocks more swift?
> Hours minutes? noon, midnight? and all eyes
> Blind with the pin and web, but theirs; theirs only,
> That would unseen be wicked? Is this nothing?
> Why then the world, and all that's in't is nothing.
>
>   (I.ii.284–93)

The unfortunate Camillo, called upon to poison Leontes' suspected friend Polixenes, is unable to counter the charges with any precision. More than likely, Polixenes and Hermione did most of the things Leontes claims to have seen. It is their intention which is the issue. Here, Leontes converts their innocence into guilt, and his conviction of their guilt is beyond penetration. As Camillo later tells Polixenes, no oaths that Polixenes could swear would possibly 'shake/ The fabric of his folly, whose foundation/ Is pil'd upon his faith, and will continue the standing of his body' (I.ii.428–31). One stage beyond Posthumus, Leontes does not even request proof. All proof points the other way, but his distorted faith refuses to hear it.

In the accusation-scene, it is in effect two types of 'faith' that contend with each other, as Leontes' conviction of his queen's guilt collides with the trust of his counsellors in her innocence, which Leontes describes as their 'ignorant credulity [which] will not/ Come up to th'truth' (II.i.192–3). In the next scene, Paulina demonstrates Hermione's new-born baby's resemblance to Leontes, but to no avail. As she rightly says, he fails to produce 'more accusation/ Than [his] own weak-hing'd fancy' (118–9). Those who now oppose him become 'traitors' and they protest in vain to be given 'better credit' and that they have 'always truly served [him]'. In the trial itself, Hermione at passionate length pleads her own pure life, and then, when her evidence is spurned, protests that she is 'condemn'd/ Upon surmises, all proofs sleeping else/ But that [his] jealousies awake' (III.ii.111–13). Finally, when the oracle, which Leontes had consulted only to silence the doubters, gives its verdict of Hermione's innocence, he refuses to hear even this proof: 'There is no truth at all i'th'Oracle:/ The sessions shall proceed: this is mere falsehood' (140–1).

By its insistent play upon the ideas of faith and proof, *The Winter's Tale* intensifies the stress *Cymbeline* implicitly puts on a rightful and proven trust. The only vestige in this play of moral experiment is in the use of a disguised Duke motif, in Polixenes' spying on his son (interestingly, he also uses that key word of the experimenter's vocabulary, 'intelligence' [IV.ii.38,46]). In this play Shakespeare has apparently moved beyond the need to take specific issue with new drama. Rather, he seems intent on stating with maximum force his own counterstatement. Again, as with *Cymbeline*, there are pagan gods and an oracle fulfilled. In this later play, Shakespeare is at some pains to point out the holiness and awesomeness of the site of Apollo's oracle, in a specially devised scene. Again, the index of a character's virtue is his faith in and submission to the will of the gods. Paulina expresses that faith from the very beginning of her persecution:

> There's some ill planet reigns:
> I must be patient till the heavens look
> With an aspect more favourable

(II.i.105–7)

Leontes' enlightenment, is expressed in terms of a whole-hearted religious penitence:[11]

> Apollo, pardon
> My great profaneness 'gainst thine Oracle
>
> (III.ii.153–4)

It is a penitence which he maintains for a whole generation, with daily prayers at the chapel where Hermione – he believes – lies; a holiness so insistent that it becomes an issue with his subjects, who urge him that he has already 'perform'd a saint-like sorrow' (V.i.1–2), and that true holiness consists in remarrying, in order to give the kingdom an heir. Yet, Leontes needs little persuasion by Paulina to convince him to hold true to the letter of Apollo's oracle, declaring the kingdom to be without a successor till his lost child be found. To an unusual extent, the whole play evolves as the fulfillment of a holy purpose, rather than having its holy purpose discovered in the conclusion. Even comparatively minor characters such as Antigonus, bearing the baby Perdita and about to be shipwrecked and eaten by a bear, seem automatically to express their own goodness in terms of a religious faith. If the heavens frown, says Antigonus, 'Their sacred wills be done' (III.iii.7).

The outstanding instance of the virtue of faith comes, however, in the bringing to life of the statue of Hermione. From the beginning, the scene is conducted in silence and awe.[12] Leontes comments on the 'magic' of the statue. Perdita prays that she not be thought superstitious, but she must 'kneel and then implore her blessing' (V.iii.44). Finally, Paulina declares to her rapt audience that she will indeed make the statue move, but tells them, 'It is required/ You do awake your faith' (94–5). While we do have a naturalistic explanation for this resurrection of Hermione – Paulina had been visiting this chapel 'twice or thrice a day, ever since the death of Hermione' (V.ii.105–6) – Paulina refuses to offer it (though Hermione herself later does). Instead, she speaks in the most pious terms: to Hermione, 'Bequeath to death your numbness; for from him/ Dear life redeems you' (V.iii.102–3); to Leontes, 'her actions shall be holy, as/ You hear my spell is lawful' (104–5). Hermione herself, in her first words, says, 'You gods look down,/ And from your sacred vials pour your graces/ Upon my daughter's head' (121–3). Leontes continues the scene's pious tone with his reference to the heaven-directed marriage of Florizel and Perdita, and to his own former wretched suspicion of the 'holy looks' (148) between Polixenes and his wife.

Clearly there is more to this scene than a mere charade dressed up in pious robes. With the whole play so much preoccupied with issues of belief, this scene seems rather to signify the final stage of Leontes' transformation from one wicked type of 'faith' to a benign and spiritual one. To doubt a known worth is clearly seen as sinful, as 'diseas'd' (I.ii.297). The cardinal virtue, the one furthest opposed to the idea of experimental tampering, is faith. Only with it comes 'grace'. That word occurs with some frequency in the play, from the joking references in I.ii, just before the emergence of Leontes jealousy (80, 99, 105), onwards. The word is lost until the beginning of Act IV, where the chorus refers to Perdita being 'grown in grace' (24), and it is she who, gracelike, supplants the winter (associated with sin and grief) with Spring (V.i.15). Yet, the ultimate grace-bringer is Hermione, in the statue-scene. Once she was, as Leontes says, 'as tender/ As infancy and grace' (V.iii.26–7). Now, 'redeemed' to life, she returns to call down 'graces' (122) in her turn.

In *The Tempest*, Shakespeare truly comes full circle from *Measure for Measure*. There is, as in the earlier play, a presiding intelligence. Like, say, Bosola, he has been drawn to abstruse learning, and by now is the complete master of his 'art'. He even boasts a full apparatus of 'utensils' (III.ii.94). Prospero, however, is no experimenter. He exercises his power on human material only because he is called to do so by Fate

> By accident most strange, bountiful Fortune,
> (Now my dear lady) hath mine enemies
> Brought to this shore; and by my prescience
> I find my zenith doth depend upon
> A most auspicious star, whose influence
> If now I court not, but omit, my fortunes
> Will ever after droop.
>
> (I.ii.178–84)

His intervention is thus almost compelled, and of course, though far more powerfully endowed than any Flamineo or Vindice, he uses his 'art' entirely benignly. If at first he looks like an avenger, answering storm with storm, shipwreck with shipwreck, and if, like any deposed duke in disguise, one of his objectives is to oust the usurpers, Prospero is in reality interested neither in revenge nor power. As to the latter, while he formally demands his dukedom back from his brother, what he looks forward to in Milan is a retirement, 'where/ Every third thought shall be my grave' (V.i.310–11). As to the former, while he many times dwells on his past wrongs, what his 'project' eventually aims to achieve is peace, forgiveness, and renewal, symbolized in the marriage of his own daughter to the son of his former enemy Alonso.

Once again, therefore, and perhaps more conclusively this time, we have a kind of anti-experimental play. All the ingredients are there, to make tampering easy: corrupted nobles, jealousy and rivalry, a chaste woman. Even without tampering, human nature is tending towards its basest, in Antonio and Sebastian's plot to murder Alonso, or in Trinculo and Stephano's sodden and bestial league with Caliban to murder Prospero. Yet, Prospero's 'rough magic', calling fools into a circle, seeks to baffle, to humble, and to disarm wickedness. As to chastity, so far from testing it, Shakespeare enthrones it. Making only token trial of Ferdinand's qualities as husband for Miranda, less as a genuine test than because 'this swift business/ I must uneasy make, lest too light winning/ Make the prize light' (I.ii.453–5), Prospero's whole design here is to bring pure to matrimony his ideal chaste young people. It is in fact Ferdinand who first mentions chastity as a requirement: 'O, if a virgin,/ And your affection not gone forth, I'll make you/ The queen of Naples' (I.ii.450–2). Prospero merely continues this concern, with his cautionary curse on their marriage, should Ferdinand 'break her virgin-knot before/ All sanctimonious ceremonies may/ With full and holy rite be minister'd' (IV.i.15–17), and his advice not to 'give dalliance/ Too much the rein' (51–2).[13]

It is precisely their innocence that Prospero most values. Their courtship as such is almost non-existent, since there are no urbane barriers in either of them to immediately confessing what they feel. Rather, 'at the first sight/ They have chang'd eyes' (I.ii.443–4), and it is finally Miranda who, against convention, but in 'plain and holy innocence', proposes to Ferdinand: 'I am your wife, if you will marry me' (III.i.82, 83). Ferdinand's act of humility, a prince bearing logs, is further proof of innocence.

Prospero's intervention diminishes with the progress of their love, but the love is from the start autonomous. Their affections and their purity are entirely their own. Prospero's function and Ariel's is merely to bring them within sight of each other. His grim-sounding aside on Ferdinand's first entry – 'The Duke of Milan/ And his more braver daughter could control thee,/ If now 'twere fit to do't' (I.ii.441–3) – implies that he does not in fact choose to exercise his control. His trust is well-placed. When, having been left together for a whole Act, Ferdinand and Miranda are revealed to the assembled interlopers at the end of the play, they are discovered *'playing at chess'* (V.i.171), a symbol as charming as passionless. Even more strikingly than in *Pericles*, with its emblem of Marina intact in a brothel, chastity is irrefrangible, and apparently central to Shakespeare's thinking. It is not simply a younger generation which regenerates an older one in *Pericles*, *The Winter's Tale*, and *The Tempest*, but a younger generation which proves its capacity to redeem the sins of its elders by an extraordinary sexual purity. When so many experimental plays insist that fidelity, or sexual purity, or sexual guardianship are comically vulnerable to the slightest trial, Shakespeare's last plays seem more and more designed as a whole-hearted counter-statement, aimed directly against one of experimental drama's central truisms.[14]

The other marked feature of these late plays' themes which is distinctly counter-experimental, the stress on faith, is again found in *The Tempest* as in the other three.[15] Again, this theme is centred on the young couple, especially Miranda. Apart from her innocence, her most marked feature is her incuriosity, again the very opposite to experimental inquisitiveness. Particularly marked here is her demeanour during Prospero's long exposition of his tribulations. It is an account he has often started, but never till now completed. Miranda is hearing it for the first time. Yet, apparently, unlike any more normal child, this is not a story she has badgered her father to hear. As she says, 'More to know/ Did never meddle with my thoughts' (I.ii.21–2). Now that the time has come, Prospero has to repeatedly interrupt his narrative to make sure she is attending – 'Mark me . . . Dost thou attend me? . . . Thou attend'st not . . . I pray thee mark me . . . Dost thou hear?' Part of this, of course, is his own agitation. Yet, Miranda hears his life's tragedy as no more than a 'tale' (106), which she hears with an almost vacant wonder. Her very name, Miranda, a thing to be wondered at, associates her with the act of marvelling, and this is what she in turn inspires in Ferdinand. Seeing her, he exclaims, 'O you wonder!', and describes himself as he 'that wonders/ To hear thee speak of Naples' (I.ii.429, 435–6). Learning her name, he bursts out, 'Admired Miranda!/

Indeed the top of admiration!' (III.i.37–8). When Prospero puts on his masque, he can tell his youthful audience, 'No tongue! all eyes! be silent!' (IV.i.59), and he is obeyed; winning from Ferdinand a tribute to his 'wonder'd father' (123). The extraordinary fresh passiveness of the couple is typified by Miranda's line, the most famous in the play, 'O wonder . . . O brave new world,/ That has such people in't!' (V.i.181–5).

At this point, where youth is brought in purity to matrimony, and when protective parenthood is able so far to purge the fallen world as to make it match the innocent and idealistic vision of youth, Prospero's presiding intelligence can abdicate its powers, break its staff. His beautiful speech on how 'we are such stuff/ As dreams are made on; and our little life/ Is rounded with a sleep' (IV.i.156–8) is, far more than Vincentio's similar speech in *Measure for Measure* on mankind having 'nor youth nor age,/ But, as it were, an after-dinner sleep,/ Dreaming on both', a sincerely held conviction, not a local tactic. It is, however, to minds quite untainted with either weariness or cynicism that he seems about to bequeath his function, and this play, more than any other of the last comedies reflects Shakespeare's determination completely to reverse the 'experimental' cycle of turning innocence into evil. Instead, evil is reclaimed, and made to serve innocence, in all its piety, passive wonder, and chastity. It is his last and most moving rebuttal of the Jacobean drama of moral experiment.

Conclusion

All the playwrights that we most prize from the Jacobean period, for their powerful, non-formulaic drama, were drawn to either endorse or contest the drama of moral experiment. There are perhaps two great names who could never be claimed among the group: Jonson and Middleton. Neither playwright is notable for his sentimentality. Indeed, both are notable for considerable sardonic harshness in their descriptions of the human condition, and therefore in a sense would seem likely recruits to a drama which deals in moral subversion and easily demolished consciences. However, the fact that both wrote drama which is almost without exception satiric is probably our best clue as to why the drama of moral experiment attracted neither dramatist. For the satirist, the immoral possibilities are already too well-known. The satirists' plots simply devise ingenious new revelations of the known and well-tried formula that the 'world's divided into knaves and fools'. The protagonists of this kind of drama – invariably its opportunists, rather than its fools – will share their authors' convictions. The last thing we can expect them to possess is any sense of curiosity in what they are engaged in. Volpone or Face, knowing human nature well, are dealing with the predictable. They assume that all who enter their trap are greedy fools, ready to be expoited, and expoitation is all they ever attempt. The only imponderables are chance accidents. The last thing a Jonsonian hero ever expresses is surprise; nor do the narratives promote it, since 'human nature' is taken to be a base constant. Not that there is no virtue in Jonson's world. Celias and Bonarios can indeed be found. The interesting thing is that this virtue, too, is a constant. There is certainly no question of a virtuous person falling, or of an exploiter finding himself capable of more complex evils. Of course, the *apparently* virtuous do very much fall. This is the very stuff of a Jonsonian plot, where a preacher or a judge is discovered to be as rapacious as the next man. Yet, the 'discovery' is always remarkably unsurprising. We come to the play as a knowing audience, savouring in advance the outrages to be wreaked, and only hoping that they prove to be theatrically satisfying.

The nearest Middleton comes to Jonson's plots of some kind of 'magnetic' fraud is perhaps *Michaelmas Term*, and the gambling-den/

usury scheme by Quomodo to strip Easy of his lands. Interestingly, the plot involves an apparent city-comedy variant on the 'disguised duke' theme, with Quomodo feigning death, and observing his own funeral, to see how well he is loved. Naturally, he discovers that he is detested. The difference from 'experimental' drama is, however, enormous. What we are watching is not the dismay of an enquirer who had every reason for a well-founded faith in his dear ones, but a richly deserved comic demise, of an established villain, whose wife's understandable liking for Easy we the audience had already seen. The other comedies, whatever their satiric trappings, and however sardonic their tone, are basically romantic comedies in their plots of true lovers contriving that their course of love will eventually run smooth. Tricks abound, but there are no experiments. It might be thought that the tragedies, since they deal so much in moral surrenders, might qualify as morally experimental. Yet, the essential quality of the plays is not enquiring, since, as in all satiric drama, the human material is again known to be base. Middleton's special territory is sexual commerce, and *Women Beware Women* is full of sexual purchase. It involves a niece incestuously accepting her uncle, and a wife trapped and seduced under threat by a Duke. Neither process is exploratory. The former is particularly intriguing here, since Isabella happily commits adultery to sleep with her uncle, when tricked into believing he is not really her uncle; while the uncle is willing to kill the sister who procured his niece for him, on the grounds that the sister's private life had compromised the family honour, when she took a commoner as her lover. This is not moral enquiry so much as moral incomprehension. In a play where aside is as prevalent as conversation, where most words have private meaning, and where the key word is 'stranger', it is clear that the play and its action are driven entirely by private and obsessional impulse. There is simply no question of any character possessing the rational detachment, the 'intelligence' in any sense, necessary to any enterprise of enquiry.

With *The Changeling*, there is, intriguingly a chastity test. Alsamero is no doting fool, and carries with him a portable apparatus for testing his wife-to-be. The contents of the Glass M produce unvarying symptoms of virginity. If they are absent, the woman is no maid. In this, the best of Middleton's plays, our interest is still, however, not quite in an enquiry of how a chaste maid (Beatrice-Joanna) may be experimented on. Rather, Middleton explores, though with more complexity, the same basic territory as before.

Beatrice-Joanna is another moral ignoramus, believing that she can dispose of an inconvenient suitor by a contracted murder, and then live happily ever after with her Alsamero. The contract killer (De Flores) in his turn is another version of the sexual-obsessives that so frequently populate Middleton's plays.[1] Driven by that obsession, he undertakes murder rather more matter-of-factly than he does his other 'service'. There is no question of discovery here; and Middleton's interest in Beatrice-Joanna's final submission to the killer into whose hands she delivers herself has all the marks, not of any form of curiosity, but of a punitive satisfaction, as De Flores insists that she is 'the deed's creature'.

We can suspect, then, that the satirist is basically too closely akin to the various common faces of his own persona – moralistic, or sardonic – to find moral experiment even remotely appealing. That is, he either perceives himself so much as a moral force within a deplorably corrupt human scene that he could entertain no interest in discovering yet murkier immoral possibilities; or he sees himself as the disillusioned, cynical observer, convinced that human nature can have nothing new to offer, and therefore once again resistant to the very idea of moral change. Add to that the satirist's preference for easily-denounced 'humours' and stereotypes, in contrast with the drama of moral experiment's evident assumption that human 'character' is infinitely elusive and unstable, and we have the curious fact that, though the plays of moral experiment contain many characters with identifiable 'satiric' character-traits (Vindice, Malevole, Flamineo *et al.*), plays of moral experiment seem almost never to be written by satirists. The exception is Marston, a writer of so little artistic self-knowledge that he can mistake the subversive for the pious.

In the end, what makes the drama of moral experiment so challenging and exciting is exactly what the satirists seem to find so alien about it: that is, its sense of a sudden and drastic new extension of what human nature is capable of. They discover that the very concept of fixed character seems awry. Marston's identity-games here are the most obviously exploratory, since his protagonist in *The Malcontent* seems so readily to be able to slip in and out of alternately high-minded and foul-mouthed roles. However, in terms of the slipperiness of the self, Webster's Flamineo and Bosola, so intent on trying to find moral lines in themselves beyond which they will not go – and so obviously failing to find them – contain far more shock value. Finally, the protagonists of both these plays and, say, *The Revenger's Tragedy* or *The Widow's Tears* or *Measure for Measure*, make their protagonists curiously probe into what they can trick, manipulate or simply persuade *others* to do. Those others may include a high-minded deputy. More likely, they will be a 'widow', a mother, a wife. These are the areas where most faith might reasonably be placed. Therefore, these are the very areas which present the most irresistible temptation to the experimenter. Here is where his proofs of how little meaning moral limits and natural 'laws' really have will be most telling. Either way, whether the experimenter is discovering if he can indeed kill his brother without scruple, or whether his mother can be persuaded to prostitute his sister, the experiment is almost invariably successful. The hilarious laughter that accompanies his discoveries is the natural hilarity of protagonists and dramatists who now discover that an entire traditional moral vocabulary is a groundless fraud. It is on the basis of entirely re-drawn assumptions that Ford can finally come along and re-write that vocabulary, making pious seem degenerate, and vice versa. The quest for moral disorder was entirely successful. The experiments duly yielded their fascinating results. There was nothing of comparable excitement happening in any part of Europe, in any other literary medium at the time.

Notes

INTRODUCTION

All quotations from Shakespeare plays are taken from the Arden editions. All quotations from other plays analysed are from the Regents Renaissance Drama editions, with the exception of *The Duchess of Malfi* (Revels).

1. George Whetstone, The Dedication to *Promos and Cassandra* in G. Gregory Smith (ed.), *Elizabethan Critical Essays*, 2 vols (London, 1904) vol.I, p. 59.
2. Michael Montaigne, *Essays*, trans. John Florio, ed. Henry Morley (London, 1893) pp. 409–10.
3. Ibid. ('Apologie of Raymond Sebond', Book II, ch. 12) p. 304.
4. Ibid. ('The Inconstancie of our Actions', Book II, ch. 1) p. 167.
5. Irving Ribner, *Jacobean Drama: the Quest for Moral Order* (London, 1962). See also R. Ornstein, *The Moral Vision of Jacobean Tragedy* (Madison, Wis., 1960). In the 1970s there were some notable interpretations of individual plays as 'absurdist': see J. R. Mulryne, 'Webster and the Uses of Tragi-comedy', in Brian Morris (ed.), *John Webster* (London, 1970). Two more recent books have self-explanatory titles indicating themes antithetical to the idea of these plays' orthodoxy: Nicholas Brooke, *Horrid Laughter in Jacobean Tragedy* (London, 1979); and Jonathan Dollimore, *Radical Tragedy* (Chicago, 1984). On the other hand, Rowland Wymer, *Suicide and Despair in the Jacobean Drama* (New York, 1986) titles his chapters, 'Retribution', 'Repentance, Expiation, and Honour', and 'Lucrece figures', and his whole interpretation favours the morally positive.
6. *King Lear*, V.iii.306–7.
7. Christopher Marlowe, *Doctor Faustus*, Act III, Chorus, ll. 1–4.
8. Ibid., II.i.143–51.
9. *Measure for Measure*, I.iii, end.
10. Ann Bartone, 'The King Disguised', in Joseph B. Price (ed.), *The Triple Bond* (Philadelphia, 1975) p. 93, sees some anticipatory hints of 'exploratory and quixotic' motive in late Elizabethan versions of the disguised ruler.

1: CHAPMAN

1. In C. H. Hereford and Percy Simpson (eds), *Ben Jonson*, 10 vols (Oxford, 1925) vol.1, p. 141.

2. *The Revenger's Tragedy* II.ii.5.
3. Thomas Marc Parrott (ed.), *The Plays of George Chapman: the Comedies,* 2 vols (repr. New York, 1961) vol.II, p. 757.
4. *The Countess of Pembroke's Arcadia,* Book I, chs 5–7.
5. As long ago as 1935, Paul V. Kreider, *Elizabethan Comic Conventions as Revealed in the Comedies of George Chapman* (Ann Arbor) pp. 80–4, noticed a great advance in cynicism between early and late Chapman comedy. He specifically compares the figure of Tharsalio in *The Widow's Tears* with that of Cleanthes in *The Blind Beggar of Alexandria,* showing that in the later play the cynic is proved right.
6. At either end of IV.ii.
7. *Bussy D'Ambois,* I.ii.224.
8. Robert Lordi (ed.), *Bussy D'Ambois* (Nebraska, 1964) pp. xxvii–xxviii.
9. Peter Bennett, *George Chapman: Action and Contemplation in his Tragedies, Salzburg Studies in English,* 8 (1974) p. 141, sees the play as one of 'ethical experiment'. This, however, is a view of some rarity, as is even Millar Maclure's impression of the play's ambiguity (*George Chapman: a Critical Study* (Toronto, 1966). More common is the insistence that the play is an either favourable or hostile study of Bussy's virtue, or *virtu*. The various critical stances along these lines are neatly summarized in Robert Lordi's Introduction to his 'Regents Renaissance Drama' edition of the play, pp. xxiii–xxx. See also Richard Waddington, *The Mind's Empire: Myth and Form in George Chapman's Narrative Poems* (Baltimore, 1974).
10. *Bussy D'Ambois,* V.i.7, 11.

2: DISGUISED DUKES: *THE MALCONTENT* AND *MEASURE FOR MEASURE*

1. For an account of the tradition of *virtuous* disguised dukes as King Arthur figures or Haroun-al-Rashid figures, see W. W. Lawrence, *Shakespeare's Problem Comedies* (New York, 1931) pp. 215 etc. For the relevance of Severus, and for parallels in contemporary political theory (Elyot *et al.*), see J. W. Lever's Introduction to his Arden Edition of *Measure for Measure* pp. xliv–li. Parallels between Shakespeare's and Marston's disguised dukes have been identified from Hazlitt onwards. Mary Lascelles, *Shakespeare's 'Measure for Measure'* (New York, 1953) pp. 25–8, conveniently draws together the evidence, mentioning also Marston's *Antonio and Mellida* and *The Fawn,* and Middleton's *The Phoenix.* The latter two seem exclusively virtuous manipulators; though Morse Allen, *The Satire of John Marston* (New York, 1965) describes how Faunus 'deliberately and in cold blood' intensifies and worsens the follies he observes, and Ejner Jacob, *Themes and Imagery in the Plays of John Marston* (Ann Arbor, 1965) p. 30, describes the same character as a 'disinterested presenter of a series of case studies'. Both descriptions tend to suggest something of the nature of an experimenter–manipulator figure even in this

later, lighter play. For an interesting real-life parallel to such figures, see Charles H. McIlwain (ed.), *Political Works of James I* (Cambridge, Mass., 1918) p. 33, and his description of a king as 'a daily watchman over his court'.

2. The following interpretation of *The Malcontent* is substantially taken from my article in *Essays in Criticism*, XXIV (1974) pp. 261–74: '*The Malcontent* and "Dreams, Visions, Fantasies"'.

3. Philip J. Finkelpearl, *John Marston of the Middle Temple* (Cambridge, Mass., 1969) p. 187.

4. *The Pattern of Tragicomedy in Beaumont and Fletcher* (Hamden, Conn., 1952) p. 67.

5. *The Malcontent*, p. xxi.

6. R. A. Foakes, *Marston and Tourneur* (Harlow, Essex, 1978) p. 31, comments on his 'delight in his own intelligence'.

7. op. cit., p. 185. The problem of role and character is astutely handled in Michael Scott's excellent book, *John Marston's Plays: Theme, Structure, and Performance* (London & Basingstoke, 1978). Scott comments that 'only once do we get any possible impression that beneath the act there is a character' (p. 31).

8. *Jacobean Dramatic Perspectives* (London, 1972) pp. 32–3.

9. R. A. Foakes, op. cit., p. 31. bluntly calls the combination 'revolting'.

10. The phrase is the title of Finkelpearl's chapter on *The Malcontent*, op. cit.

11. Op. cit., p. 24.
    George L. Geckle, *John Marston's Drama* (New Jersey, 1980) p. 84, insists that the conclusion is ironic, 'showing the ethical consequences of what happens when men . . . exceed the *lex talionis*'.
    G. K. Hunter, in his 'Regents Renaissance Drama' edition of the play (Nebraska, 1965) p. xviii, attempts to circumvent the ethical issue, by arguing that the play is 'ritualistic, not ethical'.

12. See my article, 'Old Marston or New Marston: The *Antonio* Plays', *Essays in Criticism*, XXV (1975) p. 367.

13. Rosalind Miles, *The Problem of Measure for Measure: a Historical Investigation* (New York, 1976) p. 180, comments on the coldness and neutrality of Vincentio's demeanour.

14. Numerous commentators have found parallels here with James I's distaste for the mob. See e.g. Howarth, 'Shakespeare's Flattery', *Shakespeare Survey*, 18 (1965) pp. 29–37.

15. The best analysis of this disguise, the expectations it would have aroused, and Shakespeare's distinctive handling of it, is to be found in Rosalind Miles, op. cit., pp. 167–75.

16. The most famous and influential interpretation of the play in terms of religious allegory is by Roy Battenhouse: '*Measure for Measure* and the Christian Doctrine of the Atonement', *P.M.L.A.*, LXI (1946) pp. 1029–59. The proposition is vigorously contested by Howard Cole, 'The "Christian" context of *Measure for Measure*', *J.E.G.Ph.*, LXIV (1965) pp. 425–51. Many years ago, Sir Edmund Chambers concluded, 'surely the treatment of Providence is ironic': *Shakespeare: A Survey* (London, 1925) p. 215.

17.　　See especially S. Nagarajan, '*Measure for Measure* and Elizabethan Betrothals', *Shakespeare Quarterly*, XIX (1963) pp. 115–19.

18.　　On the issues of justice, mercy and divine office, see Elizabeth M. Pope's important article, 'The Renaissance Background of *Measure for Measure*', *Shakespeare Survey*, 2 (1949) pp. 66–82.

3: *THE REVENGER'S TRAGEDY*

1.　　This view is something of a rarity in interpretations of *Rev. Trag.* Una Ellis-Fermor, *The Jacobean Drama* (London, 1936) p. 153, sees the play as a 'definite affirmation of evil'. T. B. Tomlinson, 'The Morality of Revenge: Tourneur's Critics', *Essays in Criticism*, X (1960) p. 143, argues that it 'constantly modifies traditional attitudes'. Both in a sense suppose that 'traditional' revenge plays are morally innocuous. Worse still are those interpretations which assume that even this version of the revenge play is written to uphold conventional standards, yet such interpretations abound. Examples might be Philip J. Ayres' insistence, *Tourneur: 'The Revenger's Tragedy'* (Southampton, 1977) p. 30, that 'Vindice deserves the punishment he is given. To a Jacobean audience his must have seemed a particularly vicious kind of vengeance'; or Peter B. Murray's interpretation of the play, *A Study of Cyril Tourneur* (Philadelphia, 1964) p. 223, as a delineation of the 'damnation' of Vindice; or Samuel Schuman's theory, *Cyril Tourneur* (Orono, Maine, 1977) p. 100, that by attacking sinners, the revenger thinks he can eliminate sin, yet his attack itself is sinful'.

2.　　The authorship of this play is the most vexed of any major play of the period. The major contenders are Cyril Tourneur – the traditional attribution – and Thomas Middleton. The literature on this issue is voluminous, and still inconclusive. The history of the pro-Middleton case is summarized in Samuel Schoenbaum, *Middleton's Tragedies: a Critical Study* (New York, 1955) pp. 153–82. More recently, David Lake, *The Canon of Thomas Middleton's Plays* (London, 1975), makes powerful new claim for the same author. There still remain many believers in Tourneur's claims, mostly on the grounds of the complete dissimilarity of type of play from anything else Middleton wrote. This is the view this study takes (see Conclusion for the issue of 'satire' as against 'experiment'). If Tourneur's own claim – in the light of the dissimilarity of *The Atheist's Tragedy* – seems almost equally insecure, the traditional attribution might with reservations be allowed to stand, until more conclusively demolished. Since there have been few really significant developments in the controversy more recently, Lawrence J. Ross's Introduction to his 'Regents Renaissance Drama' edition of the play still serves as a helpful summary of the major issues (Nebraska, 1966). So also MacD. P. Jackson, *Studies in Attribution, Salzburg Studies in English*, 79 (1979) pp. 33ff..

3.　　Coburn Freer, *The Poetics of Jacobean Drama* (Baltimore, 1981) p. 73, stresses how the verse itself conveys the sense of a process 'enormously satisfying to Vindice himself'.

4. Lee Bliss, *The World's Perspective* (New Brunswick, 1983), has a fascinating examination of the topic of 'The Art of Distance' in Jacobean drama (chs 2 & 3).

5. Sarah P. Sutherland, *Masques in Jacobean Tragedy* (New York, 1983) p. xiii, concludes that the masque, being 'at once "tied to the laws of flattery" and "treason's license", . . . yok[ing] violently together the decorum inherent in celebrating court entertainment with the indecorum of madness, mayhem, and murder . . . is the product of – and illuminates – a peculiarly Jacobean sensibility'.

6. Nicholas Brooke, *Horrid Laughter in Jacobean Tragedy* (London, 1979) p. 18, argues that Castiza's later pretence of having 'fallen' – a device to test her mother's newfound penitence – really consists of her 'discover[ing] the whore within herself'.

7. Brooke's whole chapter on the play, ibid., pp. 10–27, advances the proposition that 'Tourneur was a very accomplished comic dramatist'.

8. See John Peter, *Complaint and Satire in Early English Literature* (Oxford, 1956) pp. 255–87; or Irving Ribner, op. cit., pp. 72–86.

9. Freer, op. cit., p. 95, comments on how Vindice is 'excited by evil'.

10. See Peter Lisca, '*The Revenger's Tragedy*: A Study in Irony', *Philological Quarterly*, XXXVIII (1959) pp. 242–51.

4: THE WHITE DEVIL

1. Gunnar Boklund, *The Sources of 'The White Devil'* (Uppsala, 1957). See also R. W. Dent, *John Webster's Borrowings* (Berkeley and Los Angeles, 1960).

2. Harold Jenkins, 'The Tragedy of Revenge in Shakespeare and Webster', *Shakespeare Survey*, 14 (1961) p. 49. See also Roma Gill, '"Quaintly Done": a Reading of *The White Devil*', *Essays and Studies*, n.s. 19 (1966) p. 42.

3. See J. R. Hurt, 'Inverted Rituals in *The White Devil*', *J.E.G.Ph.*, LXI (1962) pp. 41–7.

4. Lee Bliss, *The World's Perspective* (New Brunswick, 1983) p. 96, calls it 'maddeningly experimental'.

5. Noted by J. W. Lever, *The Tragedy of State* (London, 1971) p. 81.

6. See J. R. Mulryne's comment that 'Familiar stage-situations and stage-conventions are also treated in a vein of parody . . . [and therefore the play's] pedigree of feeling, if not of form, can be better traced through comedy than through tragedy' (Introduction to his 'Regents Renaissance Drama' edition of the play, p. xxii).

7. It is worth noting that Flamineo is entirely Webster's importation into the original story. There is only the faintest mention of any such person in any of the sources.

8. For the Webster editor F. L. Lucas (*Works*, London, 1927, vol.I, p. 226), courage is the play's cardinal virtue, and possessed by Vittoria. For Travis Bogard '*The Tragic Satires of John Webster*' Berkeley and Los Angeles, 1955) p. 149, Webster's protagonists 'buffet their course

against a black panorama', but in their 'integrity' (a phrase which he uses to denote a quality of defiant consistency), they cut across the traditional evaluations of good and evil'; this 'integrity' proves in the final synthesis to be 'the sole standard of positive ethical judgement in the tragedies'.

At the extreme opposite end of criticism come the comments of D. C. Gunby, *Webster: The White Devil* (London, 1971) p. 58: 'It is upon the biblical commandments, upon the laws handed down from God to Moses, that the moral fable which is *The White Devil* rests'; and Vittoria's sole claim to our sympathies is that 'she is prepared . . . to acknowledge her sins' (p. 59). Other critics more sensibly detect a balance of attitude implied in the title, and see that balance enacted in our responses to both Vittoria and Flamineo. See especially two excellent essays: B. J. Layman, 'The Equilibrium of Opposites in *The White Devil*: a Reinterpretation', *P.M.L.A.*, LXXIV (1959) pp. 336–47; and R. W. Dent, '*The White Devil*, or Vittoria Corombona?', *Renaissance Drama*, IX (1966) pp. 179–203. Finally, there are those who deny that the central characters are indeed compelling. Bliss, op. cit., pp. 128–9, argues at length that, since the true control of every situation lies with Francisco, Flamineo and Vittoria are always kept at an ironic distance from us, and that, in the final unmaskings, 'which both . . . had so assiduously tried to avoid, . . . neither . . . could be farther from our sympathies'.

9. See John Russell Brown, 'The Papal Election in *The White Devil*', *Notes and Queries*, IV (1957) pp. 490–4.

10. R. W. Dent, (ed.), *The White Devil*, op. cit., p. 193.

11. Ian Scott-Kilvert first voices a widely echoed view that, by showing Isabella's murder in a dumb-show, Webster successfully diffuses the sympathy which would otherwise accrue to her (*John Webster, Writers and their Work*, no. 175., London, 1964 pp. 19–20).

12. For an overall treatment of the absurd in the play, see J. R. Mulryne, 'Webster and the Uses of Tragicomedy', in Brian Morris (ed.), *John Webster* (London, 1970) pp. 131–56. In the same volume, Peter Thomson ('Webster and the Actor' pp. 22–44) points out the sheer amount of laugher within the play.

13. For a completely contrary view, see R. W. Dent, *John Webster's Borrowings*, op. cit., p. 138: 'Flamineo is of all characters the most deceived'. But see Mulryne's view, op. cit., p. 145, of Flamineo as the '*least* deceived character in a world of false appearances' (my italics).

14. Clifford Leech's extraordinarily durable *John Webster: a Critical Study* (1951) stresses, throughout, the idea of the role-playing of all the major figure. See especially pp. 49–52 for the combination of role-playing and voyeurism: the latter being not too far removed from the impulse of experimentation.

15. J. R. Mulryne, Introduction, op. cit., pp. xxv–vi.

16. Gunnar Boklund (*Sources*, op. cit., p. 177) comments on the 'smugness' and 'impracticality' of the virtuous voices of the play.

17. Nicholas Brooke (*Horrid Laughter*, op. cit., p. 34) feels that her performance 'reveals an imagination her "pure" innocence should not possess'.

18. I am here indebted to A. J. Smith, 'The Power of *The White Devil'*, in Brian Morris (ed.), op. cit., p. 88.
19. Smith's whole article (pp. 69–92) ably argues this position.

5: THE DUCHESS OF MALFI

1. See Catherine Belsey's view, *The Subject of Tragedy: Identity and Difference in Renaissance Drama* (London and New York, 1985) p. 199, that the 'affective ideal' of love and marriage is 'glowingly defined' here. Contrast what Anders Dallby, *The Anatomy of Evil: a Study of John Webster's 'The White Devil'*, Lund Studies in English, 48 (1974) pp. 148, 163, rightly calls the 'willed family disruption', the 'deliberate perversion of values' of the earlier Webster play; or what Frederic O. Waage, *'The White Devil' Discover'd: Backgrounds and Foregrounds to Webster's Tragedy* (New York, 1984) p. 81, refers to as the 'whore-obsession' of most Jacobean drama.
2. Probably the most unqualified applause for the Duchess comes in James P. Driscoll, 'Integrity of Life in *The Duchess of Malfi'*, Drama Survey, 6 (1967) pp. 42–53. Driscoll compares her with Christ and Socrates and claims that 'the marriage of the Duchess to Antonio is a crowning act of personal integrity. It arises from real feeling'.
3. Frank Wadsworth, 'Webster's *Duchess of Malfi* in the Light of some Contemporary Ideas on Marriage and Remarriage', *Philological Quarterly*, 35 (1956) pp. 394–407; Gunnar Boklund, *'The Duchess of Malfi: Sources, Themes, Characters* (Harvard, 1962). See also James L. Calderwood, *'The Duchess of Malfi:* Styles of Ceremony', *Essays in Criticism*, 12 (1962) pp. 133–47. Such critical accounts far outweigh William Empson's flippant defence, 'Mine Eyes Dazzle', *Essays in Criticism*, 14 (1964) pp. 80–6.
4. See also Clifford Leech, *Webster: 'The Duchess of Malfi'* (London, 1963) p. 49: 'a vacillation of attitudes is . . . induced in the play; [and is] Webster's chief claim to major status in this play'.
5. Joyce E. Peterson, *'Curs'd Example': 'The Duchess of Malfi' and Commonwealth Tragedy* (Columbia and London, 1978) p. 78, convicts her of 'placing her private desires above her public responsibilities'.
6. Nicholas Brooke, *Horrid Laughter in Jacobean Tragedy* (London, 1979) p. 58, argues that she is a whole succession of roles: 'oppressed sister, oppressed woman, and happy housewife'.
7. Lisa Jardine, *Still Harping on Daughters* (Sussex, 1983) p. 91.
8. Ibid., p. 91.
9. J. R. Mulryne, 'Webster and the Uses of Tragi-comedy' in Brian Morris (ed.), *John Webster* (London, 1970) pp. 131–56, argues that the Duchess is truly her brothers' sister; and that, 'by acts of choice and by eddies of temperament [she] is firmly knit to the world that destroys her' (p. 153).
10. See Hereward T. Price, 'The Function of Imagery in Webster', *P.M.L.A.*, LXX (1955) pp. 717–39; and C. W. Davies, 'The Structure of *The Duchess of Malfi'* English, XII (1958) pp. 89–93.

11.   This point is ably made by Boklund, op. cit., p. 169, who describes her heroic death as being 'of strictly limited pertinence'.

12.   See T. F. Wharton, '"Fame's Best Friend": Survival in *The Duchess of Malfi*, *Salzburg Studies in English*, 95 (1980) pp. 18–33, for this source (25–6).

13.   Wadsworth, op. cit., p. 405.

14.   Wharton, op. cit. The chapter up to this point is based on this article.

15.   See Robert Ornstein, *The Moral Vision of Jacobean Tragedy* (Madison, Wis., 1965) p. 144.

16.   Nigel Alexander's 'Intelligence in *The Duchess of Malfi*', in Brian Morris, (ed.), op cit., pp. 93–112, misses the point, treating the concept as only pertaining to the penetration of specific secrets.

17.   This is in line with John Russell Brown's remark that, financially, 'there is almost nothing he wants'. See Brown's Introduction to his Revels Plays edition of *The Duchess of Malfi*, p. li.

18.   My interpretation is here at odds with Ralph Berry, *The Art of John Webster* (Oxford, 1972) p. 139, who sees Bosola's role-playing as basically self-protective; and with that of Lee Bliss, *The World's Perspective* (New Brunswick, 1983) pp. 140, 169, who interprets Bosola as a 'passive witness', and as a character who 'recedes' in Act V.

19.   See Coburn Freer's pertinent comment here on Bosola's 'tinkering nature' (*The Poetics of Jacobean Drama*, Baltimore, 1981, p. 168). See also Jane Marie Luecke's distinction between the Duchess and Bosola: the Duchess 'is never . . . striving to find herself in relation to ethical absolutes', whereas, 'More than any other person in the play, Bosola is the individual who "desires to find himself" in the mystery of life' ('*The Duchess of Malfi*: Comic and Satiric Confusion in a Tragedy', *Studies in English Literature*, 4 (1964) pp. 276, 280). Sister Luecke's version of Bosola's quest of self-discovery differs from my own only in her emphasis on the ingredient of ethical struggle.

6: '*TIS PITY SHE'S A WHORE*

1.   This is substantially the argument of Clifford Leech, *John Ford and the Drama of his Time* (London, 1957) pp. 41–64.

2.   George Frank Sensabaugh, *The Tragic Muse of John Ford* (New York, 1965) p. 185, argues that Ford's interests in contemporary psychology, and in coterie love codes produce an unusually dispassionate interest in moral non-conformity, and that his plays demonstrate his moral curiosity. For Sensabaugh, '*Tis Pity* 'makes an open problem of incest, and then queries the Christian idea of retributive justice'; Ford supports his challenge to an accepted morality 'by immutable scientific standards' (190).

3.   See Cyrus Hoy, '"Ignorance in Knowledge" in *Dr. Faustus* and '*Tis Pity She's a Whore*', *Modern Philology*, LVII (1960) p. 145 ff., for an account of Giovanni's intellectual self-abuse.

4. See Larry S. Champion, *Tragic Patterns in Jacobean and Caroline Drama* (Knoxville, 1977) pp. 193–4, on Putana and Vasques as 'self-serving representatives of the decadent society which comprises the background to the protagonists' destructive passion'.

5. See Mark Stavig, *John Ford and the Traditional Moral Order* (Madison, Wis., 1968) p. 107, for an account of Soranzo as 'Platonic lover'.

6. H. J. Oliver, *The Problem of John Ford* (Melbourne, 1955) p. 89, argues the Friar's moral cowardice. Others have been still more severe: for instance M. Joan Sargeaunt's comment, *John Ford* (London, 1935) pp. 124–5, that he is 'either a complete knave or a complete fool'.

7. On the play's 'catastrophic revenges', see Stavig, op. cit., p. 114.

8. For further parallels with Chapman's Herculean Bussy, see Nicholas Brooke, *Horrid Laughter in Jacobean Tragedy* (London, 1979) p. 115, n.1.

9. Many times noticed. See for instance Oliver, op. cit., pp. 86–8.

10. As Sensabaugh points out, op. cit., p. 187, their love is 'pure, according to coterie standards'. See also Ian Robson's view, *The Moral World of John Ford's Drama, Salzburg Studies in English*, 90 (1983) p. 104, that we see 'nobility, sincerity, and integrity in the lovers'.

11. See George Herndl's description, *The High Design: English Renaissance Tragedy and the Natural Law* (Lexington, 1970) of Giovanni as 'wonderful and terrible' in this last scene.

12. Dorothy M. Farr, *John Ford and the Caroline Theatre* (London, 1979) p. 55, sees Giovanni as 'rebel and iconoclast . . . yet borne forward and sustained by the conviction of his own integrity'. She also has interesting things to say about Ford's parallel *theatrical* experimentation.

13. See Ronald Heilbert, *John Ford, Baroque English Dramatist* (Cambridge, 1977) p. 55, whose view is that Giovanni 'consciously invites the death sentence', as the lovers 'isolate themselves ever more irretrievably from the natural and social orders' (96).

14. Contrast Ian Robson's denial, op. cit., p. 93, that the lovers have 'learned anything'; or Mark Stavig's detection, op. cit., p. 105, of a 'progressive degeneration' in the lovers. By normal standards, of course, both comments are true, but as Juliet McMaster helpfully reminds us, 'Central figures in any work of the imagination, if their motivation is fully and adequately worked, will always capture our sympathy, whether or not they have our moral approval' : 'Love, Lust, and Sham: Structural Patterns in the Plays of John Ford', *Renaissance Drama*, 2 (1969) p. 164.

7: SHAKESPEARE

1. Terence Hawkes' book, *Shakespeare and the Reason: a Study of the Tragedies and Problem Plays* (New York, 1965), details the Renaissance neo-Platonist preference for the perception of the intuition, rather than that of the reason (see esp. pp. 22–7). In Hawkes' discussion

of *Othello*, it is Othello's failure of intuitive perception which is stressed: in this failure, he 'allows Iago to manufacture his own world of cause and effect, and to lead Othello into it' (p. 105); and 'in murdering Desdemona, Othello murders a whole realm of "holy" non-rational belief'.

2. This translation of *de Consolatione Philosophiae* is Chaucer's ('Boece'). The section quoted is from the end of Book II (Metrum 8). See F. N. Robinson (ed.), *The Works of Geoffrey Chaucer*, 2nd edn. (Oxford, 1957) pp. 340–1.

3. Wilson Knight, 'King Lear and the Comedy of the Grotesque', in *The Wheel of Fire . . . With Three Additional Essays* (New York, 1957) p. 162, specifically identifies Lear's failure as 'a fault of the mind'. He sees Lear's condition as 'greatness linked to puerility'.

4. 'The union of Cordelia and France indicates the acceptance of her intuitive value, by a sympathetic mind open to conviction by "faith"' (Hawkes, op. cit., pp. 167–8). Hawkes also registers (p. 173) Lear's descent into merely 'scientific' modes of mathematical computation.

5. See Huston Diehl's important article, 'Horrid Image, Sorry Sight, Fatal Vision', *Shakespeare Studies*, XVI (1983) pp. 191–204, on the Renaissance view of perception as 'not merely a physical act [but] a moral act as well (p. 191). For Diehl, Macbeth illustrates 'a failure to understand the moral dimension of what he sees . . . [whereupon] the fantasy tempts him'. Thereafter, Macbeth lives only among illusions (p. 198). Diehl interestingly cites Aquinas' view that demons have only an erratic knowledge of the future.

6. See Joan Hartwig, *Shakespeare's Tragicomic Vision* (Baton Rouge, 1972) for her sustained attention to Shakespeare's stress on wonder in these plays. Of the many interpretations of their connection with religious faith, see Howard Felperin, *Shakespearean Romance* (Princeton, 1972) ch. 5, for an intelligent demonstration of their connections with Medieval religious drama.

7. Geoffrey Hill comments on this wager as an example of 'a kind of naivete which asks to be devoured, and a natural partly conscious collusion between the deceiver and the deceived': '"The True Conduct of Human Judgment": Some Observations on *Cymbeline*', in D. W. Jefferson (ed.), *The Morality of Art: Essays Presented to G. Wilson Knight by his Colleagues and Friends* (New York, 1969) p. 25.

8. Robert Grams Hunter, *Shakespeare and the Comedy of Forgiveness* (New York and London, 1965) p. 152, remarks that 'by agreeing to a test of love, Posthumus has offended against love . . . [which is] too important to risk destroying by admitting the possibility of its destruction'.

9. See Douglas L. Peterson, *Time and Tide and Tempest* (San Marino, 1973) pp. 108–50, on the issues of 'proof' and nature in the play.

10. Hunter, op. cit., p. 190, point out the absence of even that stock device, the calumniator, to give Leontes' jealousy any plausible motivation. Of course, however unmotivated, Leonte's jealousy is highly plausible in every other respect.

11. Contrast J. H. P. Pafford's comment in his Arden edition of the play (London, 1963 p. lxxiii), that Leontes displays a 'humility [which is] an unavoidable bare minimum in the circumstances'.
12. See Hartwig, op. cit., p. 135, for the sense of wonder in this scene.
13. We may also note Prospero's banishment of Venus and Cupid from his masque, since they 'thought to have done/ Some wanton charm upon this man and maid,/ Whose vows are, that no bed-right shall be paid/ Till Hymen's torch be lighted: but in vain' (IV.i.94–7).
14. Robert B. Pierce, '"Very Like a Whale": Scepticism and Seeing in *The Tempest*', *Shakespeare Survey*, 38 (1985) pp. 167–74, treats the play as a Montaignean essay in misperception, but stresses the instinctive perception by Ferdinand and Miranda of each other's fitness (p. 170). Drama is of course the perfect medium for such an enquiry into illusory perception.
15. See Howard Felperin's ideas on 'Demystification and Remystification in *The Tempest*' in Carol McGinnis Kay and Henry Jacobs (eds), *Shakespeare's Romances Reconsidered* (Nebraska, 1978) ch. 4.

8: CONCLUSION

1. See, for instance, J. R. Mulryne's description of the protagonists as 'egotists to the point where the moral sense undergoes paralysis': *Thomas Middleton* (Harlow, Essex, 1979).

Index

afterlife, 55, 63, 68, 79, 82–3, 106–7
Antonio's Revenge (Marston), 34–6
As You Like It (Shakespeare), 113

Battenhouse, Roy, 39n.16
Belsey, Catherine, 74n.1
Berry, Ralph, 89n.18
Bliss, Lee, 47n.4, 58n.4, 59n.8,
    89n.18
Boethius, 113, 115
Boklund, Gunnar, 57n.1, 72n.16, 75
bonds, human, 113–17
Brooke, Nicholas, 3n.5, 54
Burbage, Richard, 31
Bussy d'Ambois (Chapman): first pro-
    duced, 5, 16; integrity takes
    offensive in, 7; plot and themes,
    16–22; character of Bussy, 17–21

Cervantes Saavedra, Miguel de: *Don
    Quixote*, 9
Champion, Larry S., 97n.4
Changeling, The (Middleton), 106,
    108, 134–5
Chapman, George: and innocence,
    7; see also *Bussy d'Ambois*; *Gentle-
    man Usher, The*; *Widow's Tears, The*
chastity: testing of, 4–5, 9–15, 23,
    45–6, 111–12, 119–22, 134–5;
    exalted in *The Tempest*, 130–2
Chaucer, Geoffrey, 14, 113n.2
Coke, Sir Edward, 94
Coriolanus (Shakespeare), 114–15
courage, 103
Cymbeline (Shakespeare), 119–27

Davenant, Sir William, 91
deaths, absurd, 104
Dekker, Thomas, 91
Dent, R.W., 57n.1, 62

Diel, Huston, 117n.5
disfigurement motif, 7–9
disguise: in Chapman, 9–10; in
    Revenger's Tragedy, 52–3; in *The
    Duchess of Malfi*, 86–7; in *Cym-
    beline*, 133–4; *see also* dukes, dis-
    guised; role-playing; identity,
    insecurity of
Doctor Faustus (Marlowe), 55, 105
Dollimore, Jonathan, 3n.5
Don Quixote (Cervantes), 9
Donne, John, 2; 'The Good-Mor-
    row', 106
Dryden, John, 114
Duchess of Malfi, The (Webster): satire
    in, 29; and *Measure for Measure*,
    42; family theme in, 74–5, 80, 87;
    character and death of Duchess
    in, 76–87, 90; on salvation and
    afterlife, 82–3; pitilessness in,
    85–7; Bosola's motives and
    actions in, 85–90; and *'Tis Pity
    She's a Whore*, 105–6; and trans-
    cending limits, 135
dukes, disguised, 5: in Marston,
    23–36, 42–3; in Shakespeare, 23,
    36–43, 130

Edwards, Thomas, 4
Elizabeth I, Queen, 5
enquiry, in Bussy d'Ambois, 18, 20–1
evil, 3, 31, 51, 64, 83, 85, 89, 119,
    125, 132; *see also* innocence
experimentation, experimenters, 4–
    5: in *Measure for Measure*, 5, 38,
    41–2, 110; in *The Widow's Tears*, 10,
    15; in *Bussy d'Ambois*, 18; in
    Revenger's Tragedy, 45-7; in *White
    Devil*, 64–5, 68; with evil in
    Duchess of Malfi, 86–7, 89–90; and

falsification in *Cymbeline*, 119–21, 125; and satire, 133, 135

faith, 46, 85, 110, 117, 121–3, 125–9; *see also* fidelity; chastity

family, 3, 46–7, 58–9, 65, 74–5, 80, 87, 88; destruction of, in *The White Devil*, 65–9; *see also* incest

farce, absurdity, 3n.5, 53–4, 65, 68, 104

Farr, Dorothy, M., 109n.12

fate (fortune), 19–21, 96, 107

Faustus, Doctor (character), 4, 35, 105

Felperin, Howard, 119n.6

fidelity, 107–8, 111–12; *see also* faith; chastity in testing of

Finkelspearl, P.J., 30, 32

Foakes, R.A., 31n.6, 34n.9

Ford, John: dates, 5, 91; and moral disorder, 136; *see also* '*Tis Pity She's a Whore*

fortune *see* fate

Freer, Coburn, 47n.3, 54n.9, 89n.19

Geckle, George, L., 35n.11

Gentleman Usher, The (Chapman), 7–8

Gill, Roma, 58n.2

Glapthorne, Henry, 91

God: references to, 21; in *The Revenger's Tragedy*, 54–5; in '*Tis Pity She's a Whore*, 96

grace, 129; allegory of, in *Measure for Measure*, 39–41

Hamlet (Shakespeare), 1, 47, 58

Harburg, Joan, 119n.6

Harris, Bernard, 28

Hawkes, Terence, 111n.1

heaven *see* afterlife

Heilbert, Ronald, 109n.13

hell *see* afterlife

Henry IV, part I (Shakespeare), 114

Herbert, George: *Man*, 2

Herndl, George, 108n.11

Horace: 'Integer Vitae', 80–1

Hunter, G.K., 35n.11

Hunter, Robert Grams, 121n.8

hypocrisy: in '*Tis Pity She's a Whore*, 99

identity, insecurity of, 2–3, 42, 51–3, 71, 89

incest: in '*Tis Pity She's a Whore*, 93–7, 99, 101, 105–6

innocence: existence accepted, 6–7; lacks direction in *White Devil*, 72–3; in *Duchess of Malfi*, 85, 90; in '*Tis Pity She's a Whore*, 104, 106–8; and wit, 93; in *Much Ado About Nothing*, 113; in *The Winter's Tale*, 127; in *The Tempest*, 130–2

intelligence: in *Duchess of Malfi*, 86, 90; in *The Winter's Tale*, 127: lack of, in '*Tis Pity She's a Whore*, 97–8, *see also* wit

irony, dramatic, 55, 79

James I, King, 5, 39n.14, 23n.1, 110

Jardine, Lisa, 78

jealousy, 111, 126

Jonson, Ben, 6, 133

Julius Caesar (Shakespeare), 113

Kernan, Alvin, 36

Killigrew, Thomas, the younger, 91

King Lear (Shakespeare): on human bond and love, 3, 113–7; and *Duchess of Malfi*, 82; on importance of faith, 110; good and evil in, 126

Kirsch, A.C., 32

Kyd, Thomas see *Spanish Tragedy, The*

Lake, David, 45n.2

law: references to, in *The White Devil*, 62

Lawrence, W.W., 23n.1

Layman, B.J., 59n.8

Leech, Clifford, 70n.14, 75n.4, 91n.1

Lordi, R.J., 20

Luecke, Jane Marie, 89n.19

Lyly, William, 80

Macbeth (Shakespeare), 115, 117–19

Malcontent, The (Marston): first produced, 5; disguised duke and role-playing in, 23–36, 42–3, 135; Webster's Induction, 31; and evil, 113

Maclure, Millar, 20n.9

Marlowe, Christopher see *Doctor Faustus*; *Tamburlaine*

marriage: in *Duchess of Malfi*, 74–6, 78

Marston, John: and innocence, 7; conservatism, 23–4; satire in, 29, 34, 135; naive righteousness in, 34–6; see also *Antonio's Revenge*; *Malcontent, The*;

Measure for Measure (Shakespeare): moral experiment in, 5, 110–11, 129, 136; disguise in, 23, 36–43, 124; on life as dream, 132

metaphysical poetry, 2

Michaelmas Term (Middleton), 133–4

Middleton, Thomas, 91, 105, 133–5; see also *Changeling, The*; *Michaelmas Term*; *Women Beware Women*

Miles, Rosalind, 38n.13, 39n.15

Montaigne, Michel de, 1–3

Much Ado About Nothing (Shakespeare), 4, 112–13

Mulryne, J.R., 3n.5, 58n.6, 65n.12, 78n.9

nature: disconcerted by broken bonds, 115–17

Oliver, H.J., 102n.6

Othello (Shakespeare), 110–13, 121–2

Ovid: *Metamorphoses*, 4, 9

Pericles (Shakespeare), 131

Peterson, Joyce, E., 76n.5

Petronius: *The Satyricon*, 9

Pierce, Robert B., 131n.14

Pope, Elizabeth, 41n.18

Promos and Cassandra (Whetstone), 39, 42

proof, danger of, as substitute for faith, 111–13, 121, 122–3, 127

religion: in *Duchess of Malfi*, 76; in *'Tis Pity She's a Whore*, 100, 107

revenge, 44–5, 55, 57–60, 68–9, 100, 103

Revenger's Tragedy, The (Tourneur): first produced, 5; on world's knaves and fools, 6; experimentation in, 10, 136; and *The Malcontent*, 24; plot and themes, 44–56; theatre imagery in, 47–9, 65; and *The White Devil*, 57–60, 65; and salvation, 82

Ribner, Irving, 3n.5

Richard III (Shakespeare), 11, 17–18, 114

Role-playing: in *The Revenger's Tragedy*, 47–9; in *The White Devil*, 68, 69–71; in *The Duchess of Malfi*, 77, 87

Romeo and Juliet (Shakespeare), 106

Rowley, William, 91

satire, satirists, 29, 133, 135

Satyricon, The (Petronius), 9

Schoenbaum, Samuel, 45n.2

Scott, Michael, 35

self, as ultimate condition, only certainty, 63, 65, 68, 72–3, 80

Seneca, 28, 49; *Thyestes*, 29

Sensabaugh, Frank, 93n.2

Shakespeare, William: moral conservatism, 23–4, 110–11; on life and lease, 114; see also *As You Like It*; *Coriolanus*; *Cymbeline*; *Hamlet*; *Henry IV, part I*; *Julius Caesar*; *King Lear*; *Macbeth*; *Measure for Measure*; *Much Ado About Nothing*; *Othello*; *Pericles*; *Richard III*; *Romeo and Juliet*; *Tempest, The*; *Titus Andronicus*; *Troilus and Cressida*; *Winter's Tale, The*; see also faith, proof

Sidney, Sir Philip: *Arcadia*, 8

Smith, A.J., 73ns.18, 19

Spanish Tragedy, The (Kyd), 44, 47, 55, 57–8, 105

Stavig, Mark, 98n.5

Sutherland, Sarah P., 47n.5

Tamburlaine (Marlowe), 105

Tempest, The (Shakespeare), 110, 129–32

theatre imagery, theatrical blocking, etc., 25, 33, 47–8, 55, 57–8, 70–2;

see also role-playing
Thyestes (Seneca), 29
'Tis Pity She's a Whore (Ford): date of,
  91; exploration in, 91–2; wit in,
  92–3; incest theme, 93–7, 99, 101,
  105–6; plot and characters, 97–
  101, 103–9; hypocrisy in, 99;
  character of Friar in, 100–3; innocence in, 104, 108; borrowings
  and sources, 105; courage and
  cowardice in, 100, 102–3, 108
Titus Andronicus (Shakespeare), 80
Tourneur, Cyril see *Revenger's
  Tragedy, The*
'Trial', as test, 10, 15, 64, 68
Troilus and Cressida (Shakespeare),
  110

venture, venturing, 10, 18, 47
violence, brutality, 19, 34–6, 44, 65,
  73, 84, 87, 108
virtue and ideals, 8, 133; *see also*
  innocence

Waage, Frederic O., 74n.1
Wadsworth, Frank, 75
Waith, Eugene, 31
Webster, John: induction for *The
  Malcontent*, 31; collaborates with
  Ford, 91; see also *Duchess of Malfi,
  The*; *White Devil, The*
Whetstone, George, 1; see also
  Promos and Cassandra
White Devil, The (Webster): sources,
  57–9; attractive villain in, 59; plot
  and themes, 59–73; on hell, 83;
  absurd death scene, 104
Widow's Tears, The (Chapman): first
  produced, 5; innocence in, 7;
  plot, 9–16; and *'Tis Pity She's a
  Whore*, 105; experimentation in,
  136
Wine, M.L., 31
Winter's Tale, The (Shakespeare), 126–
  7
wit, 92–3
Women Beware Women (Middleton),
  104, 134
Wymer, Roland, 3n.5